Minorities and the Labor Market:

Twenty Years of Misguided Policy

Minorities and the Labor Market:

Twenty Years of Misguided Policy

Ellen Condliffe Lagemann

Richard McGahey and John Jeffries

Joint Center for Political Studies
Washington, D.C. 1985

The Joint Center for Political Studies is a national nonprofit institution that conducts research on public policy issues of special concern to black Americans and promotes informed and effective involvement of blacks in the governmental process. Founded in 1970, the Joint Center provides independent and nonpartisan analyses through research, publication, and outreach programs.

Opinions expressed in Joint Center publications are those of the authors and do not necessarily reflect the views of the other staff, officers, or governors of the Joint Center or of the organizations supporting the center and its research.

We gratefully acknowledge the support of the Bydale Foundation and the Rockefeller Foundation, which helped to make this publication possible.

Library of Congress Cataloging-in-Publication Data

McGahey, Richard.
Minorities and the labor market.

Bibliography: p.
1. Afro-Americans--Employment--United States.
2. Labor policy--United States. I. Jeffries, John, 1953- . II. Title.
HD8081.A65M34 1985 331.6'3'96073 85-19693
ISBN 0-941410-53-6

ISBN 0-941410-53-6

Printed in the United States of America

1301 Pennsylvania Ave., N.W.
Suite 400
Washington, D.C. 20004

CONTENTS

FOREWORD

Despite the recurrence over the past 20 years of policy programs designed to reduce unemployment--the War on Poverty, the Comprehensive Employment and Training Act, the Reagan administration's Job Training and Partnership Act, and, most recently, proposals for industrial policy--the rate of unemployment among blacks has consistently remained at least twice the rate among whites, during periods of economic expansion and stagnation alike. Black unemployment is particularly acute in our declining cities, where the majority of blacks live and work. And the unemployment rate for black teens has reached crisis proportions--hovering around 40 percent and above for the past several years--prompting some black leaders to endorse controversial legislation to adopt a subminimum wage for youth.

In this study, Richard McGahey and John Jeffries, research associates at New York University's Urban Research Center, examine industrial policy--the most recent in the long line of proposed approaches to unemployment. They suggest that many of the policy options that underlie the proposals have failed to curtail black unemployment because the strategies behind them are based on long-standing misconceptions about the unemployment problems of blacks. For example, one question they raise is: How useful are education and training--two staple features of these policy programs--if the real problem is not enough jobs? By analyzing industrial policy, the authors reveal a long-term conceptual problem that has impeded progress toward fuller employment for blacks.

Perhaps the most compelling statement the authors make is that blacks must get involved in the ongoing discussions. Blacks can no longer afford to sit on the sidelines during unemployment policy debates, whether the subject is industrial policy or supply-side economics or some future policy option still on the drawing table. All too often, the special concerns of minority unemployment are left out of these debates. And, as McGahey and Jeffries point out, with our society entering a high-tech and service-oriented era, the number of jobs appropriate for many blacks will probably decline. If, as McGahey and Jeffries believe, more government intervention--such as increasing public employment--will be necessary to solve the unemployment problems of black Americans, now that such approaches are coming under increasing scrutiny and criticism it is especially important that blacks get involved in the ongoing discussions.

Eddie N. Williams
August 1985
Washington, D.C.

1. INTRODUCTION

Industrial policy is the most recent in a long line of approaches to the problems of structural unemployment. Although many industrial policy ideas regarding targeted government intervention in industries are novel, in many respects the labor-market components of industrial policy proposals are quite familiar. Like conventional Keynesian policy, industrial policy emphasizes macroeconomic growth as a way of creating more jobs, and it posits education and training as the solutions to the problems of disadvantaged workers. Blacks and other minorities are seen as having quantitatively greater employment problems than white males but not qualitatively different ones. Thus, black unemployment is expected to respond to the general remedies prescribed for the economy as a whole.

We believe this line of thinking has been misguided. In this paper, we will examine industrial policy proposals in detail in order to clarify what has gone wrong with attempts to address the employment gap between blacks and whites over the past quarter-century. Of course, industrial policy is meant to address a much broader range of problems than black unemployment; in fact, the absence of attention to special minority concerns has been striking. But to the extent that the premises and strategies of industrial policy are representative of a long tradition in U.S. labor-market policy, they provide a useful case in point for confronting some common misconceptions.

We begin, in Chapter 2, with an overview of leading industrial policy proposals. These ideas focus on stimulating macroeconomic growth through a variety of targeted micro-economic strategies, all of which call for a generally increased governmental role in the economy, but few of which address the employment problems of black Americans.

We outline the employment problems of black Americans in Chapter 3 and assess various analyses of these problems in Chapter 4. The analysis we end with is the dominant explanation of the last several decades--that there has been a "mismatch" between low education and skill levels and the demands of new jobs. In Chapter 4 we also show that these analyses have dominated U.S. labor-market policy and have therefore indirectly affected blacks and the disadvantaged.

In Chapter 5, in the light of that history, we evaluate the industrial policy proposals for their efficacy vis-à-vis minorities. And we conclude, in Chapter 6, with an assessment of various policy options for improving the situation of black workers: retraining and schooling, infrastructure repair and public-service employment, and direct governmental interventions such as affirmative action and income maintenance.

2. INDUSTRIAL POLICY PROPOSALS

"Industrial policy" burst suddenly into the nation's arsenal of buzzwords around 1982 as an alternative to the apparently failing supply-side economics of the Reagan administration. Books, conferences, articles, and legislative proposals on the subject appeared, offering a host of analyses and recommending actions intended to restore American economic growth and competitiveness, all through some increased role for the government. This search for new policies was prompted by the poor performance of the U.S. economy during the 1970s and early 1980s--culminating in the deep recession of 1981-82--that was marked especially by declines in productivity, lack of international competitiveness, and the collapse of basic industries such as steel and automobiles.* Business Week (4 July 1983) summed up the concerns of industrial policy advocates:

> A decade of recessions, bouts of roaring inflation, near-depression levels of unemployment, the deteriorating competitiveness of basic industries, the painful adjustment to dependence on high-priced foreign oil, and a stagnating standard of living have shaken America's confidence in its ability to prosper and remain the world's leading industrial power. (p. 54)

---

* Some scholars deny that the United States failed to compete in the 1970s. Charles Schultze, now of the Brookings Institution and formerly chairman of the Carter administration's Council of Economic Advisors, has called industrial policy "a solution in search of a problem." But although reports from Brookings seem to suggest that the United States competed successfully even during the 1970s (Lawrence 1984), other reports continue to stress that the United States is rapidly losing its share of global manufacturing, with a real potential for permanent losses (Eckstein et al. 1984; Business Week 10 September 1984).

Between 1974 and 1978, average real gross national product (GNP) grew by 3.2 percent in Japan and 3.0 percent in West Germany and France but only 0.1 percent in the United States (Magaziner and Reich 1983, p. 12). Growth in the U.S. GNP in 1983 and 1984 was much stronger, but as we write there is some question as to how long the expansion will run. The 1984 expansion in the U.S. economy was fueled by high military spending and debt and was financed by foreign borrowing to support domestic consumption of imported goods, a pattern distressingly like that of Third World economies. The domestic economies of other countries grew faster than that of the United States, and those countries were increasingly able to penetrate world and U.S. markets, especially those of our declining basic industries. In any case, structural employment problems have continued, even during the 1983-84 economic expansion.

While industrial policy advocates agree that the United States is lagging in an important qualitative shift in the world economy (production is stagnating and international competition is rising), they recommend very different cures, many of which do not fit readily into the traditional American liberal or conservative political categories. Consider several anomalies. Liberal economist Lester Thurow, an advisor to Democratic presidential candidates and an opponent of Reaganomics, has called for increased taxation on all private consumption, thereby shifting resources to private capital investment. Leftist economists Samuel Bowles, David Gordon, and Thomas Weisskopf, all members of the Union for Radical Political Economics, offer an economic "Bill of Rights" that includes abolishing the corporate income tax and eliminating all progressivity from the income tax up to incomes of $50,000. Robert Reich, a Harvard policy analyst and leading advocate of industrial policy, says that the poor and dislocated should not bear an inordinate burden of change, but at the same time he advocates increased capital mobility, less protection for declining industries, and more rapid geographic relocation of workers. Felix Rohatyn, an investment banker at the firm of Lazard Freres who is often called an antidemocratic corporatist by leftist critics, makes a strong plea for directing capital into the declining older cities of the United States and strengthening basic industries. And William Abernathy, Kim Clark, and Alan Kantrow, professors at the Harvard Business School, blame much of the decline of American manufacturing industries not on overpaid workers or government overregulation but on private-sector managers.

To some extent, this fragmentation reflects the richness of the industrial policy debate, which is part of the larger debate over America's economic future. The dismal performance of the economy during the 1970s and the public's distrust of most of the explanations and proposed solutions helped Ronald Reagan ride into office, promising new policies supported by the "new" supply-side economics. But now all proponents of industrial policy are convinced that the United States and the world economy have entered a qualitatively new age, one in which the older policies that focused on manipulating economic aggregates (such as the level of consumer demand or the money supply) with purely cyclical policies will not be effective. Thurow put the case succinctly: "Suddenly, everyone is willing to talk seriously about a national industrial policy, and the reason is a four-letter word called fear. We all fear we may be going down for the count as an industrial power if we don't counter Japanese and European growth strategies built around industrial policies" (Business Week 4 July 1983, p. 55).

Democratic Proposals

The Democratic party was quick to adopt the term industrial policy. All of the candidates for the Democratic presidential nomination in 1984 except John Glenn supported some form of industrial policy. The Democrats sponsored several study groups on industrial policy, most notably the Senate Democratic Study Group, which produced a report entitled Jobs for the Future. The Subcommittee on Economic Stabilization of the House Banking Committee, chaired by John LaFalce (D-N.Y.), held extensive hearings on industrial policy during 1983-84, culminating in the Industrial Competitiveness Act, a bill that would have established information systems, a forum for debate on industrial policy, a bank that would make loans to advance industrial policies, and a federal industrial mortgage association (U.S. Congress 1983-84). Another House initiative that incorporated elements of industrial policy was the National Employment Priorities Act, sponsored by Congressman William Ford (D-Mich.) and others (U.S. Congress 1983). This bill would have created federal policy to deal with plant closings and community economic disruptions. (The 1984-85 session saw much less activity on these types of initiatives.)

In 1983, a constituent element of the Democratic Party, the AFL-CIO Executive Council, called for "a national industrial policy to modernize basic industries, support development of technologically advanced industry in the United States, and reverse the deterioration of public services and infrastructure" (AFL-CIO, p. 3). AFL-CIO President Lane Kirkland actively participated in a study group on industrial policy with Felix Rohatyn and former DuPont Chairman Irving Shapiro. Although Walter Mondale (1983) didn't use the term in his presidential campaign, he once called for "a new industrial policy," stressing both the revival of basic industries and the development of "high-tech" firms by targeting investment policies, increasing training and education, shifting capital into plant and equipment investment, limiting the export of advanced technology, encouraging cooperation among the sectors in adjusting to change, coordinating government programs, and aiding the communities and regions hardest hit by economic change.

Robert Reich and the "Human Capital Strategy"

Some of Mondale's ideas, especially the stress on education and training, echoed those of Harvard policy analyst Robert Reich, one of the leading proponents of industrial policy. In two books published in 1983, Minding America's Business, written with Ira Magaziner, and The Next American Frontier, Reich has offered the most comprehensive liberal critique to date of recent American economic policy, proposing a wide range of innovations to deal with American economic problems.

Reich is a committed interventionist, dedicated to increasing the speed of U.S. adaptation to economic change. He states that the United States already possesses an industrial policy, but an "irrational and uncoordinated" one encompassing trade restrictions, education and training policy, military spending, tax policies, loan guarantees, research expenditures, and social welfare payments (Magaziner and Reich 1983, p. 255). He rejects the criticism of industrial policy as unwarranted governmental interference in the free market, arguing that "in advanced industrial nations like the United States, drawing such sharp distinctions between government and the market has long ceased to be useful" (Reich 1983b, p. 5).

Like many others, Reich lays a large share of the blame for U.S. economic decline at the doorstep of American management. He claims that U.S. firms failed to adapt to a changing international economy, especially to competition posed by foreign manufacturers of high-volume standardized products. Unlike the Japanese, who shifted into specialized high-value-added products, leaving standardized products to developing countries, U.S. firms agitated for tariff and trade barriers, received a plethora of tax breaks and subsidies, and devoted themselves to "paper entrepreneurialism"--avoiding taxes, reshuffling assets through mergers and acquisitions, and manipulating accounting practices--rather than reinvest in new plants and equipment.

Reich argues that as long as U.S. wages and standards of living are far above those of the Third World, the United States will not be able to compete with developing countries in high-volume standardized production. Rather, capital and labor should be made more flexible and mobile by reorganizing management practices and production, shifting into high-value production, and training workers to be more adaptable. Reich is a strong advocate of free trade, arguing against protectionism for U.S. industries, which in the short run has shielded U.S. firms from the need to make the changes necessary for successful long-run economic health.

Reich draws a much more explicit link between economic policy and politics than many other industrial policy advocates. In the future, he believes, economic challenges will require dramatic changes in institutional and managerial practices. He calls for national wage and price policy to control inflation, but wants to increase the role of private firms in distributing costs and benefits: "Business enterprises . . . will largely replace geographic jurisdictions as conduits of government support for economic and human development. Companies, rather than state and local governments, will be the agents and intermediaries through which such assistance is provided" (1983b, p. 248). Those who make economic choices should take explicit account of the political costs, because the older managerial rigidities that pervade private and public institutions prevent necessary adjustments. "We need political institutions that are . . . less concerned with making 'correct' decisions than with making correctable ones; less obsessed with avoiding error than with detecting and correcting for error; more devoted to responding to changing conditions and encouraging new enterprises than stabilizing the environment for old enterprises" (1983b, p. 277).

Alperovitz and Faux: Community Economic Planning

Other analysts agree that American economic adjustment is constrained by an outdated image of a government that is, or ought to be, separate from economic planning. One industrial policy program that would expand local democratic economic planning is that of Gar Alperovitz and Jeff Faux. In their book Rebuilding America: A Blueprint for the New Economy (1984) they paint America as a "broker state" that is intimately involved in the economy but whose real nature is hidden from view by an outdated ideology about free-market economics. Their goal, paralleling some of Reich's ideas, is to make the public role in economics more explicit and democratic.

But where Reich would concentrate on corporations and firms as the institutional mechanisms for economic coordination, Alperovitz and Faux stress local communities. They note that the United States is a highly decentralized society, in part because of

Americans' distrust of centralized government. Alperovitz and Faux do not want to fight against this deeply rooted political culture with proposals for centralized federal policy, but neither do they wish to create investment and decision structures that are insulated from politics. Rather, they wish to build on the traditions of decentralization by providing local communities with economic planning capacity and as much control as possible over local policy.

Like other industrial policy writers, Alperovitz and Faux do not pay much explicit attention to minority economic problems. They do not fully address the problem of highly unequal resources among localities; it is not clear how their decentralized planning would equalize burdens among America's highly unequal population groups or eventually result in a national economic structure that could respond effectively to global economic change. Furthermore, state and local governments have often been poor guardians of minority rights; a decentralized strategy must avoid returning to the "states' rights" policies that have historically exacerbated tensions between blacks and whites.

Felix Rohatyn and the Revival of the RFC

The Industrial Competitiveness Act proposed by Representative LaFalce, with its National Industrial Development Bank, incorporates a policy advocated since the mid-1970s by Felix Rohatyn. Rohatyn has called for a new Reconstruction Finance Corporation (RFC) named after the New Deal bank but modeled more along the lines of the Municipal Assistance Corporation and the Emergency Financial Control Board, institutions established to oversee and control New York City finances in return for federal loan guarantees to the city during the city's fiscal crisis in the 1970s. Rohatyn also advocates tax changes to bring down deficits, including a simplified personal income tax, a minimum corporate income tax, and higher gas taxes. Better coordinated trade policies are also on his agenda, including higher exports to the Third World, which will in turn require some international loan guarantees to stretch out Third World debt repayment schedules.

Rohatyn rejects any attempt by the government to pick winners--that is, to direct funds to industries that are felt to be promising. He does want to help buffer "losers," stressing support for the victims of economic change and major investments in urban infrastructure. His ideas are heavily influenced by his experiences in New York City's fiscal restructuring, which involved nonelected bodies with budget control independent of elected officials and which also required substantial sacrifices on the part of labor unions and city residents. "When budgets have to be cut or long-standing expectations have to be revised, the blame will have to be widely shared. On a limited scale, that is what the Municipal Assistance Corporation in New York was about" (1983, p. 49). Rohatyn envisions tripartite institutions of business, government, and labor leaders making many decisions about how to distribute the sacrifices required by the new economy, leaving market mechanisms as the main source of growth and choice: "I am opposed to government planning and to government-owned industries. I believe that the free market is usually the best market" (p. 49).

Critics on the Left

The New York City model frightens critics on the left, even those who agree that more coordinated and planned economic policies are needed. Leftist economists Samuel Bowles, David Gordon, and Thomas Weisskopf find the major problems in many industrial policy schemes to be "the dangers they pose to democratic institutions" (1983b, p. 705). They view the New York City experience as a "curtailment of the democratic accountability of government bodies" and fear that industrial policy proposals like Rohatyn's, in a quest for restoring productivity and profitability to private business, will hasten economic change in ways that leave many people worse off.

Like most participants in the industrial policy debate, Bowles et al. focus on the loss of productivity in the American economy as a key issue, but rather than blame declining productivity on a shortage of investment funds, they see the slowdown as stemming from an inability of U.S. firms to impose greater work intensity on the shop floor, an expansion of the "social wage" through domestic income transfer and maintenance programs (although they feel this can be maintained while raising productivity), and the erosion of American international economic and military domination, which made imported raw materials (such as oil and minerals) more expensive. Bowles and his coauthors reject any notion that more resources should be transferred to private firms, claiming that the U.S. economy already operates with an enormous amount of slack capacity, a slack required by the irrational domination of private profit: "Useful output could have been more than $1.2 trillion higher than it was in 1980, the equivalent of 49.6 percent of useful national product in that year" (1983a, pp. 10-11). Instead, they propose a far-reaching "Economic Bill of Rights" to establish full employment and job security, cut military spending, encourage wage-led growth by pushing up income supports and minimum wages, expand education and child-care, and simplify and reduce personal and corporate taxes. The program would pay for itself through the elimination of economic waste.

A similar theme has been sounded by economists Barry Bluestone and Bennett Harrison, who criticize industrial policy advocates for concentrating too much on economic growth without paying attention to the political and social costs induced by private markets. In The Deindustrialization of America (1982), they call for a broad range of restrictions on capital mobility, including plant-closing legislation with substantial severance pay, continued health insurance for workers, and support for employee buy-outs or governmental take-overs of plants and facilities. Like Bowles et al., they do not see a capital shortage and hence see no reason for cutting consumption and social expenditures to transfer resources to the private sector. Many of the policies they suggest might be part of a more conventional interventionist strategy, especially programs dealing with plant closings, job security, and extended governmental benefits to workers displaced by economic change, but they make much more activist calls for increased workplace democracy and control over capital mobility than other industrial policy advocates.

Although their analyses and policy recommendations vary widely, all of the participants in the industrial policy debate share certain basic premises. They all start with the macroeconomic stagnation of the 1970s (Bowles et al. see it starting in the mid-1960s). Declines in American productivity, especially in manufacturing, are seen as the key to this stagnation, and American private-sector managers receive a great deal of blame for declines in basic industries. Industrial policy proponents reject supply-side and monetarist macroeconomic policies and claim to be dubious about Keynesian approaches, although their stress on the necessity of macroeconomic growth makes their rejection of Keynesian economics less than convincing. Indeed, one of the striking features of industrial policy schemes is the stress on restoring macroeconomic growth through a series of microeconomic policies aimed at specific sectors.

Minority workers are not singled out for special assistance, despite their especially straitened condition; they are generally expected to benefit like everyone else from any overall improvement in the economy. But, as we shall show in the next chapter, there are many circumstances that set black labor markets apart and deserve close attention.

3. BLACK EMPLOYMENT PROBLEMS

Before looking at how industrial policy programs might affect black employment, it is useful to review the dimensions of recent black employment problems and then (in the next chapter) to examine some of the economic analyses of those problems. (By "employment problems," we refer both to the ability to obtain jobs and to the salary and quality of the jobs that are held.)

Concern over minority employment problems has centered on the extraordinary problems of black youth; much less attention is paid to problems faced by adult black workers. But there is evidence that many problems faced by minority youth continue into adulthood. Further, the employment problems of minority youth are also directly tied to the employment problems of adults: most people find their jobs through personal networks, but minority adults often cannot provide such networks for youth. Nonetheless, it is useful to look at youth and adult employment problems separately, since many of the available data have been compiled separately.

Black Youth Employment Problems

The figures describing the employment crisis among minority youth are staggering. The unemployment rate for 16- to 19-year-old blacks was 41.7 percent in September 1984, even after almost two years of economic recovery (39.9 percent for males, 43.7 percent for females). In 1980, according to the Center for Labor and Urban Programs (1981), 46.8 percent of all teenagers in the nation were employed; but in central cities, only 39.1 percent were employed, and in New York City, just 22.0 percent. Nonwhite teenagers accounted for 44 percent of the unemployed, while they were only 30 percent of the labor force.

This problem has been building over the last several decades and cannot be explained by a worsening of the labor market for all teenagers. The history of unemployment rates for different racial groups in the work force shows that nonwhite teenagers have always had higher rates of unemployment than whites, but the gap grew during the 1970s. In New York City, the unemployment rate for young people tripled between 1969 and 1976. Table 1 shows the unemployment rates of subgroups of young black and white workers and the ratio of black-to-white unemployment rates. For black teenagers, male and female, this ratio has grown throughout the past two decades, indicating that the employment situation for young blacks has become worse relative to their white counterparts.

These persistent and widening gaps have given rise to public concern and a variety of sometimes competing explanations and theories. A simple dichotomy can be drawn between explanations that focus on structural or "demand" factors and explanations that focus on the individual or "supply" characteristics of minority youth themselves. Demand factors include the demographic impact of the baby-boom generation; the movement of blacks from the South and the decline in southern agricultural employment; the movement of jobs out of inner cities to suburbs; changes in the requirements and availability of entry-level jobs; and racial discrimination.

The supply factors are the labor-related characteristics of minority youth themselves: levels of education, training, and job experience; the increased enrollment of blacks in school (which cuts down the time they are available to work); allegedly poor work attitudes or unrealistic expectations about wages and working conditions; and participation in "underground" economic activity, such as income-generating street crime, as an alternative to lawful work.

Demand Factors

Demographic Changes. Although the large number of young people in the baby-boom generation is partly responsible for the overall decline of young workers' wages relative to older workers' wages, it does not explain the growing gap between black and white youth employment levels. As Freeman observed, "From 1969 to 1977, while white teenage employment increased, black teenage employment actually fell by 3.1 percent" (1980, p. 26). Ellwood and Wise pointed out that youth employment patterns between 1960 and 1980 varied substantially by race and sex; the growth in the gap between black and white **male** teenagers was due to declines in the black employment level, while the gap between black and white **female** teenagers grew because of employment gains by white females. They also noted that the

Table 1. Unemployment rates and ratio of black-to-white unemployment rates, by age, race, and sex, 1960-1979.

Year/ age group	Males: Percent unemployed: Blacks & other minorities	Males: Percent unemployed: Whites	Males: B/W unemp. ratio*	Females: Percent unemployed: Blacks & other minorities	Females: Percent unemployed: Whites	Females: B/W unemp. ratio*
1960						
16-17	22.7	14.6	1.55	25.7	14.5	1.77
18-19	25.1	13.5	1.86	24.5	11.5	2.13
20-24	13.1	8.3	1.59	15.3	7.2	2.12
1965						
16-17	27.1	14.7	1.84	37.8	15.0	2.52
18-19	20.2	11.4	1.77	27.8	13.4	2.07
20-24	9.3	5.9	1.58	13.7	6.3	2.17
1970						
16-17	27.8	15.7	1.77	36.9	15.3	2.41
18-19	23.1	12.0	1.92	32.9	11.9	2.76
20-24	12.6	7.8	1.62	15.0	6.9	2.17
1975						
16-17	39.4	19.7	2.00	38.9	19.2	2.03
18-19	32.9	17.2	1.91	38.3	16.1	2.39
20-24	22.9	13.2	1.73	22.5	11.2	2.01
1979						
16-17	34.4	16.1	2.14	39.4	15.9	2.48
18-19	29.6	12.3	2.41	33.4	12.5	2.67
20-24	17.0	7.4	2.30	20.8	7.8	2.67

Source: U.S. Bureau of Labor Statistics, Handbook of Labor Statistics, 1980, Table 32, pp. 67-70.

* If the unemployment rates for whites and blacks were the same, the ratio would be 1.00.

impact of the baby boom did not coincide with the most rapid falls in minority employment, and that, in general, the labor market absorbs most teenagers during the summer months (1983, pp. 6 ff.). (If the market were incapable of absorbing large numbers of youth, then summers should see dramatic increases in unemployment for **all** youth, black and white.)

Cogan (1982), who concluded that the decline in southern agriculture explained much of the national drop in the black teenage employment-to-population ratio between 1950 and 1970, did not find the rapid increase in the size of the youth population to be a factor; he also concluded that the decline in southern agriculture does not explain the declining employment situation after 1970. Osterman (1980) and Borjas (1983) deduced that white teenagers and adult females may have "crowded out" black youth from the job market, especially from the low-paying jobs, but these effects are not statistically reliable and not very large in any case. Whatever the relative effects of demographic shifts for youth as a whole, most observers do not find that demographic changes account for much, if any, of the black-to-white differential.

Suburbanization of Jobs. Some commentators have attributed black youth employment problems to a movement of jobs from central cities to the suburbs. If new entry-level jobs are being created in the suburbs, where black youth are less likely to live or commute, rising black youth unemployment may result. However, relatively little evidence supports this analysis. Harrison (1972) found that some jobs were moving but that black youth were much worse off than white youth even when both groups lived in the suburbs. Osterman (1980) likewise rejected the suburbanization explanation. And Ellwood, in a recent examination of the Chicago labor market, reported that although jobs were moving out of the central city faster than black residents were moving out, deterioration in the work experiences of black teenagers was not significantly affected by this job movement: "Black and white teenagers who live in the same neighborhood fare just as differently as blacks and whites who live across town from each other" (1983, p. 4).

Changes in Available Jobs. Osterman (1980) found evidence that job structure had shifted in ways that harmed young black men; the number of industries employing a substantial number of young workers declined in central cities, and Osterman's analysis indicated that the adverse effects of these shifts were concentrated among black males. Montgomery and Jackson (1983) reported that certain occupations and industries had higher than average job losses, and black teenagers' loss of jobs was partly due to their concentration in such volatile industries. Manufacturing, retail trade, and service industries were all found to be especially volatile. Data for New York City supported this finding: black teenage workers were concentrated in retail trade and finance sectors. However, blacks were not heavily concentrated in manufacturing, as has often been assumed. Thus, declines in the retail and finance sectors may have harmed teenagers more than the decline of manufacturing.

Discrimination. Relatively little attention has been focused on racial discrimination as a factor in growing black youth joblessness. Osterman's analysis of the black-to-white employment gap found that "residual factors account for roughly 50 percent of the unemployment differential, and it is conventional to interpret this residual as discrimination" (1980, p. 147). Culp and Dunson's (1983) experiment with black and white young job seekers holding similar credentials and with similar background characteristics ascertained that prospective employers treated blacks worse than whites.

A U.S. Commission on Civil Rights report found that discrimination was a continuing and substantial source of employment disparities: "Even when minority youths and white youths of the same age and educational attainment are competing for jobs, black and Hispanic youth are less likely to receive them" (1982, p. 58). The commission cited evidence that blacks require more education to get the same occupational returns as whites, a finding similar to the one reported by Harrison (1972), who discovered in his samples of urban area workers that white high-school dropouts received higher earnings than black high-school graduates.

Supply Factors

Education and Training. Structural explanations for the employment gap between black and white youth concentrate on differences in the characteristics of black and white workers--in economists' terms, the "supply" characteristics of labor. Principal among these factors are differences between blacks and whites in education and training, often termed "human capital" by economists. If whites hold higher levels and superior types of human capital than blacks, then whites' greater rewards in the labor market are evidence of rational market operations.

There is a vast literature on human capital differences, ranging from theoretical models to evaluations of government training programs. For examining youth employment issues, it is useful to view the effects of human capital in two ways: the effects on obtaining employment and the effects on wages and job quality. Freeman summarized this research by stating, "The factors that are associated with youth joblessness are not, it is important to recognize, the same factors that determine the wages of young workers" (1980, p. 20). According to Freeman, being black reduces the probability of finding work but not the wages received once work is found and other factors are taken into account.*

Among young minority males, Grant (1983) reported, high-school dropouts have harder transitions to work than high-school graduates. Longer stays in school are associated with higher employment probabilities, and work experience while in school also raises the probability of work once out of school. We will return in a subsequent chapter to a more extensive discussion of the impact of education and training on minority employment, when we discuss the "mismatch" hypothesis, a popular hypothesis that also applies to adults.

School Enrollment. Another factor thought to influence the decline in black youth employment is the increase in black school attendance. Between 1970 and 1982, the share of high-school graduates among blacks between the ages of 25 and 34 years old climbed from 53 to 79 percent (U.S. Bureau of the Census 1983). If more time was spent in school, then less time might have been available for work. A drop in black youth employment might be a disguised blessing if it were tied to higher school attendance, but this is not the case. Ellwood and Wise (1983) showed that employment rates for black males both in and out of school declined during the 1970s, while enrollment and employment patterns for black women hardly changed at all. Osterman (1980) attributed some of the negative effects on employment--but not a substantial part of the employment gap between blacks and whites--to increased school enrollment.

Aspirations and Work Attitudes. A third supply-side explanation for the black-to-white gap focuses on young blacks' attitudes and expectations about work. If they are demanding too high a wage for work (the "reservation wage," below which they would not work even if jobs were available) or have bad work habits or unreasonable demands for easy work, then they will suffer lower employment.

Osterman (1980) discovered no support for the view that blacks have too high a reservation wage, a finding echoed in Culp and Dunson (1983). Further, youth do not seem inordinately choosy about jobs. In Osterman's study of Boston teenagers of all races, he found that "youths generally take the first job they are

---

* This tendency toward equalization of wages is not necessarily due to human capital payoffs; it may be tied to governmental policies such as affirmative action and minimum wages.

offered" (p. 42)--in this study, 78 percent of the time. Freeman, reviewing several parallel studies, reached a similar conclusion: "Virtually no unemployed young job seeker reports having rejected a job offer during the period of search" (1980, p. 22).

Osterman also reported no support for the view that blacks have aspirations that are too high, although he admitted that his measures of aspiration were "crude" (1980, p. 146). In contrast, Datcher-Loury and Loury (1983) found that "some measures of attitudes, values, and beliefs are . . . important determinants of labor supply" in a sample of young urban minority males, as did Freeman (1983), who found that church attendance and other variables that might be considered indicators of work attitudes (the work and welfare status of family members, for example) could be significantly associated with school attendance, work, and participation in criminal and deviant activities.

Much of the attitude research is confounded by the crude measures available and by the fact that what people say about their attitudes may not reflect their behavior. For instance, Sadd, Kotkin, and Friedman, in an evaluation of the effects of labor-market programs on poor urban teenagers with substantial criminal justice involvement, reported no significant correlations between a variety of attitude measures and labor-market outcomes. They stressed, however, that some of the standardized scales provided for this Labor Department-sponsored program "appeared to lack face validity, and many did not seem appropriate to this population" (1983, p. 85).

The "Underground Economy" and Criminal Income. Another explanation for high black youth unemployment rests on the possibility that black youth have more lucrative income sources in the "underground economy," especially in criminal activity. Although this explanation is hard to test definitively, recent studies of criminally involved youth suggest that no neat trade-offs are being made between crime and employment. An analysis of the crime and employment experiences among a sample of 900 persons arrested for felonies in Brooklyn, New York, found no clear evidence of trade-offs between crime and employment, partly because the monetary returns for most street crimes tend to be very low (McGahey 1982). Sadd, Kotkin, and Friedman (1983) discovered no evidence that crime and employment functioned as income substitutes among the teenagers eligible for the program studied. And the supported work experiment of the Manpower Demonstration Research Corporation (1981) did not reduce recorded crime among its teenage participants even while they were in the program.

Most teenage crime tends to be spontaneous and unplanned, performed for short-term income needs. Crime diminishes with age, household formation, and labor-market involvement; but the reciprocal causation among these factors is much more complex than the trade-off model of economics assumes (McGahey 1981). Indeed, as Sullivan (1983) pointed out, in most cases criminal involvement precedes lawful employment by several years. There is not much reason to believe that higher payoffs in criminal activity relative to lawful work contribute significantly to higher black youth unemployment.

Thus, substantial levels of youth unemployment, especially among minority youth, cannot be adequately explained by the personal characteristics of minority teens. Clark and Summers claimed that "while instability and frequent turnover are major factors in determining the overall pattern of teenage unemployment, we find that the lack of desirable employment opportunities is the crux of the problem for those most seriously affected by youth unemployment" (1979, p. 10). Much of the unemployment problem is concentrated among among a small, disproportionately black group, who cannot locate jobs. Freeman, too, concluded that much of the youth joblessness problem was directly related to a dearth of jobs, "although the problems of the most severely affected are compounded by other social and individual factors" (1980, p. 29).

That the gap between black and white youth employment is growing remains a puzzle to most economists. Among the less convincing explanations are demographic factors, the suburbanization of employment, and the attractiveness of criminal opportunities. School enrollment plays a minor part in reduced job seeking by young blacks. Discrimination is a persistent factor in the gap between black and white teen employment. There is confusion and debate on the role of attitudes and aspirations; this body of research, still in its infancy, is fraught with methodological problems.

Another issue of concern is the long-term effect of teenage unemployment. If teenage unemployment were only a transitory phenomenon with no adverse long-term consequences, then public policy toward it might be concerned only with tiding youth over. However, Stevenson found that teenage unemployment is related to substantial problems later: "Youth labor-market status is not only related to but seems to have an effect of its own on subsequent employability and income" (1978, p. 115). Ellwood agreed that there are such effects but found them to be small. In particular, erratic early labor-market experiences are associated with later unemployment, but effects of these experiences are relatively small once the individual desire and tendency to work are taken into account. Ellwood did find a "sizeable impact" of erratic work experience on lowering wages (1979, pp. 60-61).

Black Adults: The Chronically Unemployed

The possible long-term effects of youth unemployment are mirrored in the problems of chronically unemployed adults. Clark and Summers noted that much youth unemployment is "concentrated among a relatively small, disproportionately black group who experience long-term unemployment" (1979, p. 58). A similar concentration is found among the adult unemployed. Freeman reported that many adult workers remain permanently at the bottom of earnings distributions, and that these low-earnings workers are disproportionately "black, poorly educated, relatively unskilled, female, and located in certain industries" (1982a, p. 2). Black men have increased their employment share in some occupations, while at the same time their total labor force participation rate has fallen. Black women, especially single heads of households, remain the group in the most serious trouble. The persistence for a decade or more of high unemployment rates in particular geographic areas has resulted in concentrations of distressed workers. Some cities and regions now feature a deadly combination of high unemployment and low wages.

Studies from the National Longitudinal Survey also reveal a large concentration of unemployment among a relatively small group of the adult work force. Among four different age and gender groups, 10 percent of the long-term unemployed accounted for 35 to 40 percent of the total number of weeks of unemployment (Parnes 1982, p. 54). The principal factors associated with long-term unemployment were education, occupation and industry, and race.

Describing the chronically unemployed and underemployed is easier than analyzing the causes of the problem. Freeman found it is very hard to predict who will remain in the lowest earnings group over time (1982a, p. 2). Parnes could explain only between 10 and 25 percent of the total variation in unemployment and concluded that "a substantial amount of unemployment experience appears to result either from simply being in the wrong place at the wrong time or from personality characteristics that generally go unmeasured" (1982, p. 56).*

---

* This last comment by Parnes is echoed by Freeman, who assumed that the inability to explain much of the low-earnings concentration "highlights the importance of personal unobserved factors in the labor-market problems of individuals" (1982a, p. 2). Economists are generally wedded to a theoretical outlook for understanding employment that, unconsciously or not, downplays

Black Concentration in Stagnant and Declining Industries

Despite the passage of civil rights legislation and the establishment of attendant social programs designed to integrate minorities into the economic mainstream, three facts have continued to characterize the labor-market status of blacks over the past two decades: blacks continue to have lower per capita and family incomes than whites; employed black Americans generally receive lower than average wages; and the unemployment rate for black workers is at least twice that for white workers at all points over the business cycle. Chief contributors to these continuing disparities between black and white incomes and employment rates are the disproportionate representation of blacks in lower-paying occupations, in the lower-earnings and lower-status tiers within specific occupational groups, and in the industrial sectors that are most sensitive to the business cycle. Fifteen years ago, the Kerner Commission reported:

> Negro workers are concentrated in the lowest-skilled and lowest-paying occupations. These jobs often involve substandard wages, great instability and uncertainty of tenure, extremely low status in the eyes of both the employer and the employee, little or no chance for meaningful advancement, and unpleasant or exhausting duties. . . . The concentration of Negroes at the lowest end of the occupational scale is . . . the single most important source of poverty among Negroes. (U.S. National Advisory Commission on Civil Disorders 1968, pp. 253-54)

And in the 1983 edition of the Urban League's The State of Black America, David Swinton wrote:

> Black workers of both sexes had significantly less favorable occupational distributions than did white workers. In general, black workers tended to be concentrated in the lower-paying, less prestigious occupations. Moreover, since each of the broad census categories covers such a wide range of occupations, these figures probably understate the black occupational disadvantages. (p. 65)

---

the importance of structural factors, including discrimination, in favor of explanations that rest on distributions of personal characteristics. Osterman said that it is "conventional" to interpret unexplained gaps between black and white employment as discrimination (1980, p. 147), but it is in fact far more common among economists to ascribe differences to unobserved personal characteristics.

Recent analyses of Current Population Survey (CPS) data from the U.S. Bureau of the Census on the growth and racial composition of employment during the 1970s confirm that black employment patterns have not changed significantly and in many instances have deteriorated. Diane Westcott of the Bureau of Labor Statistics' Division of Employment and Unemployment Analysis concluded from her analysis of CPS data that "black occupational advancement in the 1970s [was] not particularly impressive. . . . In most cases, black workers [in 1980] were concentrated in the same jobs in which they were employed in 1972" (1982, p. 31). Almost half of the total job growth in the economy over the nine-year period occurred in two white-collar groups--in professional and technical and in clerical occupations. Westcott noted that "although a higher proportion of blacks could be found among the professional and technical occupations in 1980 than in 1972, they were concentrated in jobs at the lower end of the professional pay scale" (p. 30).

In fact, the earnings gap between black and white professionals and technicians remained the same over the period. And although white participation in clerical and sales jobs declined while black men and women increased their participation in those fields, according to Westcott, the disparity in earnings between black and white clerical employees widened.

In the 1970s, blue-collar jobs grew more slowly than white-collar occupations and also at a slower rate than blue-collar employment expansions in previous decades. While blue-collar workers compose almost one-third of total employment, they have accounted for only one-seventh of the overall increase in job holders since 1972. Blacks participated in this downward shift: the proportion of black men who were blue-collar workers in 1980 declined from the 1972 level.

Within blue-collar occupations, black males made some moves out of undesirable operative and nonfarm laborer jobs and into the skilled craft and kindred trades. "By 1980, the largest proportion of black men in any single occuptional group was in skilled craftwork." But Westcott noted that "despite this improvement, there were still relatively high concentrations of black men in the less-skilled categories" (1982, p. 30). Compared to their white counterparts, black men were twice as likely to be laborers, and both black males and females were twice as likely to be service workers.

Black male concentration in the lower-level blue-collar occupations coupled with the overrepresentation of black women in clerical and service occupations documents the persistence of the disadvantaged status that blacks occupy in the contemporary labor market. An examination of black employment in both broad and detailed occupational groupings reveals that in the growing white-collar categories, blacks are concentrated in the lower-paying jobs where earnings gaps have often widened or at best remained constant.

In 1980, black men made up only 4.4 percent of professional and technical workers but 16.4 of all social and recreational workers, a subcategory of professional and technical employment. Black men constituted 15.7 percent of nonprivate household service workers but 22.8 percent of cleaning service employees, and 15.5 percent of all laborers but 32.8 percent of all garbage collectors.

Concentration patterns for black women are similar. In 1980, black women constituted 10.6 percent of the employed labor force. They made up 8.8 percent of professional and technical workers but 17.4 percent of social and recreational workers, and 14.6 percent of all "operators" but 40.4 percent of laundry and dry-cleaning operators. And in the growing non-household service jobs, black women constituted 15.9 percent of all workers but 30.2 percent of cleaning service workers (Westcott 1982).

The growing representation of black men in the occupational groups where employment is declining overall is equally disconcerting. The movement of some blacks into the more-skilled blue-collar jobs did not offset their continuing over-representation in lower-paying blue-collar work and has occurred over a period during which blue-collar industries, particularly manufacturing, have been plagued by both cyclical and structural decline. Even when blacks have moved into white-collar jobs, their earnings have not greatly increased and have sometimes declined. Movement into more-skilled blue-collar occupations, on the other hand, has left blacks vulnerable to economic downswings and sectoral decline.

Black unemployment rates have been at least twice those of whites throughout the post-World War II period. The two-to-one ratio applies "for blacks of all ages, both sexes, all educational levels, in all regions of the country, [in] center cities and in the suburbs" (Swinton 1983, p. 66). Black joblessness has not fallen below 12 percent since 1975, and the rate for black teenagers has hovered in the 40 to 50 percent range over the period. Black adults are currently experiencing unemployment levels greater than at any other period since the late 1950s.

Many analysts believe that blacks' concentration in industrial occupations may be responsible for the relative deterioration of black economic conditions. According to the second annual report of the Black Enterprise board of economists, "blacks . . . suffered profoundly during the [past] recession because [they] tend to work in the manufacturing sectors directly affected by slowdowns, layoffs, and plant closings." Board member Phyllis Wallace, an economist at the Massachusetts Institute of Technology, argued:

> [An increasing number of] blacks have been added to a structural base of unemployment--joblessness that results from basic changes in the way the economy works. . . . [Because] blacks were already disproportionately represented in the area . . . when the economy swings out of recession, there will be a large number of blacks who are left behind in that structural unemployment pool. It may very well be that in coming out of the recession blacks will be in a worse position than they were going in. (Black Enterprise, March 1983, p. 66)

The employment status and prospects of minorities have been further limited by the American economy's deteriorating international position. An analysis of the impact of foreign trade on domestic employment between 1964 and 1975, conducted by economists at the Bureau of International Labor Affairs, produced a ranking of the 20 most adversely and the 20 most favorably affected industries and identified workers "that benefited from increasing trade and those that were forced to bear the burden of adjustment, principally through reduced job opportunities" (Aho and Orr 1981, p. 31). The most damaged industries had an average of 11.5 percent minority workers, compared to 7.4 percent for trade-enhanced sectors. The study concluded:

> The industrial sectors that experienced the largest negative impact on job opportunities employed more women and minorities and their work forces were less educated and less skilled than industries that benefited most from trade. In addition, workers in the adversely affected industries had lower earnings and were more likely to have a family income below the poverty level than those in trade-enhanced industries. (p. 34)

Thus, nonwhite workers are concentrated in the lower-paying and less prestigious white- and blue-collar occupations; they are disproportionately harmed by recessions; and they are more adversely affected by foreign trade.

4. LABOR-MARKET THEORIES AND FEDERAL ECONOMIC POLICIES TOWARD MINORITIES

Policy analysts have long noted the problems with black employment patterns and, over the past several decades, have developed both economy-wide and individually based theories to explain the employment problems of black workers. These theories of labor-market operation developed reciprocally with economic policies, and both responded to the changing political context.

In the mid-1960s, the civil rights movement, which had originally devoted its energies to eliminating black disfranchisement and _de jure_ segregation, embarked on a new mission. Although the right to vote and social integration were recognized as necessary components of equality, black leaders increasingly felt that the "fate [of black Americans] is inextricably tied up with the American economy" (Patterson 1977, p. 155). In "From Protest to Politics," Bayard Rustin asked, "What is the value of winning access to public accommodations for those who lack the money to use them?" (1965, p. 25). A statement by Dr. Martin Luther King, Jr., shortly before his death echoed Rustin's concern: "What good is it to be allowed to eat in a restaurant if you can't afford a hamburger?" The necessary elimination of legal barriers to participation in American society in no way guaranteed that blacks would be able to obtain economic benefits. To attack the problems of black employment, poverty, and housing, Rustin and others asserted that the civil rights movement "was compelled to expand its vision beyond race relations to economic relations, including the role of education in society" (1965, p. 25).

In response to this shift in emphasis and to increasing black militance, federal policy makers aimed at integrating minorities into the economy through two related strategies. The first stressed macroeconomic growth and was based on the premise that the best way to increase the economic welfare of minorities was to expand the total pie. The second strategy was rooted in the belief that the problems faced by economically disadvantaged groups stemmed in large part from their own limitations as workers; this approach stressed human resource or manpower policy to help the disadvantaged through education and training.

These two strategies complemented each other through the belief that increasing workers' educational levels led to increased productivity and increased economic growth. Much of the economy's high levels of growth over the two decades following World War II was attributed to the rising educational attainment of the labor force and its contributions to productivity growth (Denison 1979). Solutions for the disadvantaged economic status of blacks focused on more education, better employment preparation, and macroeconomic growth. These strategies were based on the "mismatch" hypothesis and a "productivity queue theory" of the labor market.

Unemployment, Mismatches, and Queues

To understand the mismatch hypothesis and the queue theory, we must recognize three distinct types of unemployment--frictional, cyclical, and structural. "Frictional" unemployment is defined as joblessness resulting from the normal movement of people between jobs and in and out of the labor force. Individual workers search for the job that best matches their supply characteristics and desires; they are voluntarily out of work while searching. Search theory suggests that individuals are unemployed in order to engage in productive job hunting or employment preparation; some economists use it to explain why workers rationally choose to be unemployed during the course of their labor-market experience. Some argue that frictional unemployment is responsible for the majority of the economy's joblessness at any point over the business cycle and, further, that unemployment resulting from "normal turnover" generates "positive externalities by reducing recruiting costs" and therefore enhances the market's efficient operation (Hall 1972).*

"Cyclical" unemployment is defined as the loss of jobs during economic downturns or from generally inadequate aggregate demand. Because cyclical downturns are by definition temporary, the resulting unemployment will also be temporary; workers should regain their positions during the recovery. If a

* For a review and critique of this view, see Clark and Summers 1979.

worker is employed and therefore properly matched to a job before a cyclical decline, then there is no reason to assume that his or her ability to do the job or to fulfill the requirements for doing the job will change because of, or during, the downswing. The symmetry of the business cycle should help the individual regain a job as demand increases and labor markets tighten.

"Structural" unemployment is often defined as what is left after frictional and cyclical unemployment have been accounted for. In general terms, structural unemployment is the result of changes in the way the economy operates. It involves changes in the characteristics of workers and changes in the economy's industrial and occupational mix--that is, changes in the very process by which workers and jobs are matched.

Over the past two and a half decades, structural unemployment has come to have two distinct economic meanings. In the late 1950s and early 1960s, structural unemployment was defined in terms of joblessness resulting from technological displacement and automation. Twenty-five years ago, technology and automation were expected to generate a demand for increasingly sophisticated skills, which many workers did not have. The result was a broad gap between the skills demanded by employers and those possessed by workers--a structural mismatch.

The other meaning of structural unemployment came from the observation that there was an increasing concentration of joblessness among particular segments of the labor force. Despite improvements in the economy, the duration and severity of unemployment among minority, female, and young workers led to the concept of chronic, or "hard-core," unemployment. This second meaning of structural unemployment has dominated American labor policy toward the disadvantaged, through the "mismatch" hypothesis. The mismatch hypothesis asserts that individuals are out of work because they lack skills or education. (Recently, the first meaning--technological displacement--has reentered the discussion, on the premise that white-collar and high-tech jobs need higher skills.)

A related explanation of black alienation from American economic life is the "productivity queue theory" of the labor market. The queue theory describes the labor market as one in which employers rank workers according to their respective productivities. The most productive workers are at the front of the queue, receive high wages, and are most likely to be employed. The least productive, unskilled workers are at the end of the queue; they receive low wages and are often out of work. By this reasoning, the lower wages and higher unemployment rates of black workers are caused by the tendency of those workers to be less productive than white workers and thus to be put at the "back of the line."

The productivity queue vision of the labor market, coupled with the mismatch hypothesis, has supported two policy prescriptions for raising the employment status of the disadvantaged. Because the demand for labor is seen as a derived demand (labor is not purchased for its own sake; jobs come into existence because consumers are willing to spend money to purchase goods and services), it is assumed that employers ultimately hire workers in response to consumer demand. The first policy prescription, the classic Keynesian macroeconomic policy consistent with the queue theory, is an expansionist fiscal and monetary policy that generates demand for goods and services. Employers will then reach deeper into the hiring queue to meet that demand and avoid production bottlenecks and loss of business. This type of analysis is reflected in the constant stress on macroeconomic growth as a necessary prerequisite to solving the problems of the economically disadvantaged. Economist Richard Freeman summarized this view: "Reduction of poverty, . . . allocation of a greater share of desirable jobs to women and minorities and increased support of older persons is easier, most would agree, in a growing economy than in a sluggish one" (1983, p. 356). A rising tide lifts all boats.

In addition to using economic expansion to enhance the status of disadvantaged workers, labor-market policies have endorsed education and training strategies designed to move workers further ahead in the productivity queue, thereby increasing their chances of employment. This second approach is buttressed by the stress on the importance of "human capital." Gary Becker, the principal expositor of this theory, linked human capital to macroeconomic growth through "the realization that the growth of physical capital . . . explains a relatively small part of the growth of income in most countries" (1975, p. 9).

Human capital theory attempts to reconcile income distribution with the productivity queue, holding that individuals' incomes correspond to their productivity: more productive workers command higher wages. Investment in human capital enhances individual productivity and in a competitive labor market leads to increased employment and wages. Through additional investments in human capital, the economically disadvantaged (blacks in particular) could raise their individual productivity and the productivity level of the economy as a whole, fostering economic growth that would allow further increases in their piece of the pie. Such human capital acquisition would also enhance their employability and future earnings and move them up in the hiring queue, as they acquired the supply characteristics needed to obtain better paying jobs.

These theories and policy approaches have dominated during the past several decades (except when direct interventions were attempted, such as public-sector employment or affirmative action policy, which we discuss in Chapter 6). Although some of the particulars change, U.S. labor-market policy has consistently been based on macroeconomic growth and human capital theory for the last several decades. This tendency continues in current discussions, especially in much of the debate on industrial policy, as the following review of U.S. labor-market policies shows.

Labor-Market Policies Since 1960

Early Efforts: ARA and MDTA

The Area Redevelopment Act (ARA) of 1962 was passed during the Kennedy administration to stimulate growth in regions plagued by high unemployment. ARA had four principal features: (1) loans to businesses willing to relocate to or expand in economically depressed areas; (2) federal financial aid to localities for infrastructure improvement and development; (3) technical assistance to firms for the development of new products and markets; and (4) training programs for disadvantaged residents of depressed areas to assure participating businesses of a skilled labor force (Manpower Report of the President 1963, p. xvii). But the economy's inability to recover from the 1958 and 1961 recessions, the flight of younger workers from depressed areas, and the low job participation rate of the disadvantaged all contributed to the program's demise. ARA was phased out in 1965.

The Kennedy administration also implemented the Manpower Development and Training Act (MDTA) in 1962, which provided the model for subsequent manpower programs. MDTA and later amendments were directed toward retraining technologically displaced workers and enhancing the education and training of the unskilled. Levitan and Mangum (1969) summarized the four basic objectives of MDTA as (1) meeting labor shortages in specific industries; (2) providing employment opportunities for the unemployed; (3) upgrading the labor force; and (4) providing an escape from poverty.

The architects of MDTA attempted to resolve two rather different economic problems. The first was the persistence of specific industrial and technological labor shortages despite a relatively low national unemployment rate; the second was the persistence of a hard core of unemployed (even though the program was designed primarily to retrain experienced workers, who would presumably be easier to place).

Over time, it became clear that nearly all of the program's resources were being devoted to the least disadvantaged. In an attempt to resolve this problem, two-thirds of the placements were reserved for the more disadvantaged workers. The establishment of this quasi-quota has been attributed to "the earlier debates over structural vs. aggregate demand explanations of unemployment in the early 1960s and . . . continued unrest among Negroes and other minority groups"; it was justified as "a consequence [of accepting] the principle that improving the competitive position of the disadvantaged is an appropriate goal for public policy, even though it may threaten the more favorably situated" (Levitan and Mangum 1969, pp. 39, 30).

Other related initiatives included the Trade Expansion Act of 1962. While this was not formally human resource legislation, it did contain provisions for workers, and those provisions later became the rule in manpower programs. The act authorized retraining allowances, income maintenance, and funds for relocation to workers whose jobs were lost because of U.S. tariff concessions. The program was short-lived because of difficulties documenting which workers were affected, and because proponents of trade expansion policies argued that total U.S. employment was expanding, providing new job opportunities for the displaced.

The War on Poverty

By the mid-sixties, the economy began to show positive signs of recovery and growth, as the national unemployment rate fell below 4 percent. The unemployment rate for white men aged 16 years and older was 2.7 percent in 1967 and fell to 2.5 percent in 1969. But despite improvements in the economy's overall performance, the unemployment rate of blacks remained over 6 percent at a time when a national unemployment rate of 5 percent was considered catastrophic. These figures somewhat discredited the notion that economic growth in and of itself could remedy black employment problems. As a result, the mismatch hypothesis and education and training strategies targeted at the disadvantaged achieved increasing influence in human resource policy over the next 15 years.

The Johnson administration's War on Poverty and especially the Economic Opportunity Act (EOA) of 1964 constituted the new "active manpower policy." As described in the Manpower Report of the President, the program had three fundamental goals: "(1) to develop workers' abilities; (2) to create jobs which will make the most of worker's abilities; and (3) to match workers with jobs" (1969, p. 3). The first goal was in response to increasing concern with the lack of quality education among the poor. Thus, job training was supplemented with programs designed to improve education at all levels. The Adult Basic Education Program established under EOA was implemented to provide remedial education to individuals aged 18 years and older in elementary and secondary schools. Upward Bound and Talent Search were federally funded programs that provided remedial education to disadvantaged youth to help them gain college admission. Motivated ghetto students with academic potential were encouraged to seek admission to institutions of higher education.

In addition to developing individual workers' abilities, the War on Poverty sought to create jobs by attracting capital to ghetto areas in order to enhance economic development in the residential environments of disadvantaged minority workers. The Model Cities Program was designed to improve ghetto neighborhoods by rehabilitating substandard housing and providing essential community services and facilities. In 1968, President Johnson authorized an amendment to MDTA, entitled Job Opportunities in the Business Sector (JOBS), described in the Manpower Report of the President (1968) a program that would help diffuse social unrest in the ghettos. JOBS aimed to: (1) establish jobs in or near low-income areas;(2) obtain placement commitments from existing and new firms in those areas; and (3) involve the private sector in offering employment opportunities to the disadvantaged. The National Alliance of Businessmen (NAB) was charged with pledging jobs for the program, and it became known as the NAB-JOBS program (Manpower Report of the President 1968).

Matching people to jobs, the third objective of the new manpower policy, aimed at more active identification of the disadvantaged and the fine-tuning of existing labor-market mechanisms thought to connect people with jobs. The Neighborhood Youth Corps, a work-training program for younger workers aged 16 to 21, was established in 1965 to enhance the employability of youths and reduce school drop-out rates. The Job Corps, also begun in 1965, offered basic education, vocational training, and counseling to 16-21 year olds. The distinguishing feature of the Job Corps was its physical removal of young people from poverty-stricken homes and communities to other residential sites; it was believed that ghetto environments created significant barriers to becoming a productive adult.

Programs for welfare recipients included the Community Work and Training (CWT) Program, the Work Experience and Training Program, and the Work Incentive Program (WIN). CWT, an experimental effort administered by the Welfare Administration, was established in 1962 as an amendment to the Social Security Act. Designed to increase the employability of AFDC (Aid to Families with Dependent Children) recipients by letting them work off public assistance and instilling in them proper work attitudes, CWT was implemented in direct response to critics of the welfare system. The Work Experience and Training Program introduced under EOA was intended to provide work experience to "persons who were unable to support or care for their families" (U.S. Statutes at Large, 1964 1965, p. 527). The WIN program, a joint effort of the U.S. Department of Health, Education and Welfare and the Department of Labor, required that mothers with children over six years of age register with the U.S. Employment Service (USES). The minimum age for eligibility was lowered from 18 to 16 in recognition of the increasing incidence of teenage motherhood in urban ghettos. The creators of the WIN program believed that work experience was more efficient than classroom training as a way of instilling proper attitudes.

With the development of data-processing and telecommunications systems, USES aggressively sought out unemployed and discouraged workers rather than wait for them to knock on the door. In addition, USES made referrals to sponsors in the Concentrated Employment Program (CEP), established in the summer of 1967. CEP was charged with enlisting the support and commitment of local businesses and unions, developing employment opportunities suited to individual program participants, and following up on placements to decrease post-program turnover. The rationale for the coordination of CEP and USES was to avoid overlapping and inefficiencies created by previous manpower programs, which were thought to impede the successful matching of people and jobs.

The goals of human resource policy in the 1960s were greatly influenced by the new demands of civil rights advocates, but the policies framed were based on the mismatch hypothesis. With the growing recognition that a positive relationship between macroeconomic growth and black economic progress was by no means automatic, policy makers focused on altering the supply characteristics of black labor force participants in the hope of preventing immediate social unrest and reducing poverty in the longer term.

Education and training were seen by both black and white civil rights advocates and intellectuals as "the corridor through which America's minorities must travel to move from rejection, deprivation, and isolation to acceptance, economic sufficiency, and inclusion" (Proctor 1970, p. 43). This emphasis on education and training was in place as the economy began to enter the recession-ridden, slow-growth era of the 1970s. The Nixon administration's rejection of the War on Poverty and its expansion of NAB-JOBS and introduction of the Comprehensive Employment and Training Act only served to affirm the mismatch hypothesis. Even as operating policies and institutions were changed, the rationale for the programs remained unquestioned.

The 1970s: CETA

The intellectual hegemony of the mismatch hypothesis shifted debates within human resource policy from **what** should be done for the most disadvantaged to the most efficient **way** to deliver the agreed-upon services. The Nixon administration criticized the War on Poverty because of the fragmentary, and hence costly, manpower programs authorized under the expanded MDTA and EOA. Nixon's "new federalism" also suggested that not enough control had been given to states and localities, which supposedly had a much better idea of their specific problems and possible solutions to them than did the federal government. But it did not challenge the basic approaches by which the least advantaged workers were to be helped.

Under a strategy that became known as "manpower revenue-sharing" (Hewitt 1973, p. 1), federal funds for manpower programs would continue to be supplied, but the authority and responsibility for the programs would shift to state and local governments. The strategy was aimed at "pragmatic administrators seeking a more rational way to conduct employment and training activities, . . . those attracted by the features of grassroots participation, and . . . those committed to a reduction of the federal role" (Mirengoff and Rindler 1978, p. 2). After rejecting the original Nixon proposal (the Manpower Training Act of 1969), Congress finally enacted the Comprehensive Employment and Training Act (CETA) in December 1973. The "comprehensive" part of the legislation referred to the decentralization of manpower services.

But CETA was comprehensive in two other important respects, which can be traced to the productivity queue theory's influence on the legislation. Throughout its various titles, CETA was structured to implement both the macroeconomic and human capital-related recommendations that flow from the queue theory.

CETA's countercyclical component (expanding employment when the business cycle turned downward) and public-service employment (PSE) provisions were designed to help workers at the bottom of the queue by subsidizing their employment when the overall demand for goods and services was low. In December of 1974, the Emergency Jobs and Unemployment Assistance Act authorized $25 billion for countercyclical PSE under Title VI in response to the deepening recession. Under this new title, PSE was extended to all areas, not just those with unemployment rates of 6.5 percent or more as previously specified under Title II; the public sector became the "employer of the last resort."

At the same time, CETA's training components were designed to augment the human capital of the disadvantaged, preparing them for unsubsidized private-sector jobs through education and exposure to proper work habits and attitudes. Although the public-service jobs created under CETA were considered "transitional employment," the work programs authorized did not require local governments to guarantee permanent employment after PSE jobs ended.

CETA's training provisions were tied to a proliferation of income-maintenance programs. Stipends for institutional and classroom trainees and funds for support services such as counseling, medical care, and day care were considered necessary if the poor were to participate in the programs. Titles III and IV of CETA categorical programs were funded to aid groups that policy makers argued needed even more special attention, including welfare recipients, ex-criminal offenders, drug addicts, veterans, and migrant workers. The Job Corps program for youth and the Youth Conservation Corps were also funded under Title IV of CETA.

Thus, although CETA represented many operating changes, the fundamental twin thrusts of labor-market policy still applied: a focus on macroeconomic policy (through countercyclical measures) and a continued stress on training the disadvantaged. Income maintenance was provided through training stipends, but this did not result in the transformation of welfare spending to a more work-oriented policy. As the economy persisted in its stagnation, CETA programs were viewed as providing dead-end jobs that allowed local governments to bloat their payrolls. The perceived failure of CETA to provide significant numbers of permanent links to private-sector jobs led to growing discontent, culminating in federal legislation giving the private sector a central place in training policy.

JTPA and the Return to the Private Sector

The Reagan administration's Job Training Partnership Act (JTPA) represents a deliberate shift of federal employment and training policy toward the private sector. In contrast to CETA, which the new legislation replaced, JTPA does not fund public-service employment and virtually eliminates the income maintenance provisions characteristic of CETA by limiting "supportive services" spending to just 30 percent of a local program's total funding. The new act stipulates that at least 70 percent of awarded funds must be spent on training. (According to Assistant Secretary of Labor Albert Angrisani, less than 18 percent of CETA expenditures were devoted to actual training.) Employment and training programs under JTPA are valued only as a means of achieving unsubsidized employment in the private sector (Marth 1983, p. 61).

JTPA requires each local service delivery area to establish a Private Industry Council (PIC) composed of business, labor, educational, and community representatives, with a majority of the council members and council chairs from the business sector. Each PIC is responsible for developing training programs and selecting the participants, based on the PIC members' knowledge of the local labor market. (This mandate transcends the role of PICs under the Private Sector Initiatives Program established in 1978 under Title VII of CETA, which called for the formation of PICs only as "consultants" to local prime sponsors.)

The rationale for a greater private-sector presence in employment and training is based on a combination of perceptions concerning the effectiveness of CETA and its public-service employment component and the job-providing virtues of the private sector. To many, CETA symbolizes wasteful government spending, running up a bill of $53 billion in nine years without preparing participants for existing opportunities in the private sector. In a recent Nation's Business article entitled "The Job Training Partnership Act: A Victory for Business--And a Challenge," Marth wrote: "Ever since President Franklin D. Roosevelt reached into the federal treasury 50 years ago to buy a pick and a shovel for America's unemployed, business people have been contending that the solution to unemployment lies not in government largess but in the competitive, profit-motivated private sector."

A less passionate assessment of policy makers' renewed interest in the private sector was provided by Isabell Sawhill, then-director of the National Commission for Manpower Policy:

> . . . there is a feeling in many quarters that we may have overindulged in this selective [public] employment policy. In fact, many feel that public employment has taken on a life of its own, creating a kind of fiscal addiction for municipalities and nonprofit organizations. Moreover, the value of experience gained in a PSE job and the ability of participants to move into the regular economy is open to question. The result of this growing disenchantment with large-scale public-sector programs has been increased attention to new ways of moving the disadvantaged into private-sector jobs. (1978, p. 68)

According to Robert Guttman, counsel to the Senate Subcommittee on Employment and Productivity when JTPA legislation was being debated, supporters of public-service employment programs did not agree that PSE was an inefficient policy, but they decided to fight the PSE battle in a separate piece of legislation rather than endanger the passage of a bill authorizing training programs (1983, p. 6). What emerged was

JTPA, with its training focus but no new public-service employment. Again, the institutions change, but the central focus on training remains.

The fact that five out of every six nonagricultural wage and salaried workers are employed in the private sector is often cited as the compelling reason for greater emphasis on the private sector as the preferred location of job placements. Moreover, training by the private sector supposedly provides more relevant preparation for unsubsidized jobs than programs developed and operated by the public sector, because training is administered by those most familiar with private-sector needs. Private-sector training is also thought to minimize institutional barriers to unsubsidized employment and to ease the transition from the program to work. (This role of the private sector may not be equally important for all. As we shall see, government employment has been of major short- and long-term importance for blacks.) Many advocates of private-sector involvement also claim that employment and training programs will be made more efficient through the business community's influence.

These propositions and their supporting rationales have more or less shaped employment and training policy over the last five years and led to bipartisan support for and passage of the Job Training Partnership Act. But many of the same policies that existed under CETA seem to have been followed in JTPA's first year, although with reduced funding, some shifts in the agencies contracted to do training, and more of an emphasis on short-term training and direct job placement (Cook et al. 1984; Walker et al. 1984).

Thus, in American labor-market policy toward minorities, two themes have dominated: the need for macroeconomic growth so we can afford education and training programs and the need for ways of eliminating the "mismatch" between jobs and workers via training and education. Although the programs change, the dominant ideas remain the same, in periods of growth and stagnation alike.

The stress on restoring macroeconomic growth through raised productivity is also a staple of industrial policy. Indeed, there are numerous parallels between many industrial policy ideas and the nearly 30 years of U.S. labor-market policy outlined above.

5. INDUSTRIAL POLICY, EDUCATION, AND TRAINING

Industrial policy advocates have said very little about the particular economic problems of black Americans. This failure to discuss black problems in more depth is surprising, as blacks suffer disproportionately from America's sustained economic problems and are concentrated in many of the industries that have declined during recent years. Although some of this silence can be attributed to a general rhetoric about the widespread nature of current economic problems, it also reflects the unconscious influence of the mismatch idea. Advocates of industrial policy stress retraining and education policy in the context of macroeconomic growth, in terms rather consistent with U.S. manpower policies of the past 30 years. We suspect that many industrial policy advocates would address black employment problems with education and training policies based on a mismatch explanation for black unemployment, an approach that we question.

Industrial policy programs for black employment are conditioned by the overall view of American economic and social institutions. Reich (1983b, especially chapter XI) attempts to square a traditionally American circle by claiming that social spending can foster economic growth, rather than see social programs as a deduction from national wealth, as something we can afford only if economic growth is first ensured. He argues that the new world economy will be based on more flexible production and more mobile and better educated labor. Government programs to create this flexible "human capital" will, in fact, be creating the conditions of new economic growth. Workers in changing firms can be given more training and adapted to new jobs; welfare should be replaced by grants to businesses that hire the chronically unemployed; traditional training programs and public-service employment should be replaced by vouchers that the unemployed can use to get on-the-job training at private firms. The economists to the left call for more use of affirmative action programs and community control of resources (Bluestone and Harrison endorse producers' cooperatives at the local and state level), but even their attention to minority workers is subsumed under the general problem of industrial and regional adjustment.

There are three areas in which we believe industrial policy falls short of addressing black employment problems: the nature of firms where blacks work, the role of schools and training in the labor market, and shifts in the composition and number of available jobs. In all three areas, we see a grimmer picture than many other policy analysts, and this picture makes us question much of industrial policy's current relevance to black employment problems.

Firm Size, Job Ladders, and Black Employment

Most industrial policy writing depicts a world of potential cooperation between business, labor, and government leaders, where large, politically powerful firms with unionized work forces, capital intensive production, and extensive layers of managerial personnel are battered by international competition. (Even leftists such as Bluestone and Harrison concentrate their attention on multi-site manufacturing firms with locations in many states and overseas.)

But a large part of the labor market for blacks, especially in inner cities, is made up of rather different firms and job experiences. Some economists have described a "dual" or "segmented" labor market, where distinct types of firms offer distinct types of jobs:

> The primary market offers jobs which possess several of the following traits: high wages, good working conditions, employment stability and job security, equity and due process in the administration of work rules, and chances for advancement. The other, or secondary sector, has jobs which, relative to those in the primary sector, are decidedly less attractive. They tend to involve low wages, poor working conditions, considerable variability in employment, harsh and arbitrary discipline, and little opportunity to advance. The poor are confined to the secondary labor market. (Piore 1977, pp. 93-94.)

This picture of a dual market captures an important facet of the American labor market, one to which most industrial policy writers pay little attention. Indeed, much job growth in the past decade has been precisely in firms and industries that are low-skilled and low-paying, with erratic employment opportunities (Jeffries and McGahey, forthcoming).

When Reich calls for firms to administer new programs, or Rohatyn endorses linking schools to jobs and private firms, or Bluestone and Harrison want to restrain capital mobility, they all seem to have in mind the primary sector. That is, industrial policy advocates are focusing on large firms with internal mobility through job ladders, often with unionized work forces.

They do not seem to be thinking about the small, secondary firms that provide a good deal of inner-city employment. Training and skills are not very important for workers in these firms, as they are often labor-intensive service or manufacturing firms with few skilled jobs. Benefits are marginal or nonexistent, and it is hard to imagine these secondary firms helping their displaced workers or hiring new ones from the ranks of the chronically unemployed. Perhaps industrial policy advocates hope economic growth will eventually aid these firms and workers, but this would sound disturbingly like the supply-side economists' "trickle-down" theory.*

The School-to-Work Transition

Rohatyn states, "We have all heard that high technology creates higher requirements for skills and few requirements for labor." He endorses adapting training programs and "even our education system to what we need," which might include "inner-city schools that will be more closely connected with job opportunities" (1983, pp. 46, 47).

The concern about the school-to-work link is nothing new in American policy. School-to-work transition problems are periodically recycled as a major explanation for youth employment problems. This usually leads to calls for more direct ties between jobs and school in the form of more involvement by private firms in curriculum design, ties between apprenticeship programs and schooling, or cooperative ventures in which part of the school day is spent at a private-sector job.

Osterman, however, argued that "much of the policy focus on the 'school-to-work transition' is misguided. . . . The ineffectiveness of schools is not a recent phenomenon . . . and the essential characteristics of the youth labor market make this

---

* Bowles et al. do call for raising minimum wages to force modernization in secondary firms, driving some of the least productive out of business (1983a, pp. 280-81).

inevitable" (1980, p. 154). Youth are not ready to stabilize in the labor market, and firms that provide long-term job opportunities and stability of employment do not hire them.

A recent variation of the school-to-work issue has been a refocus on improving basic skills of high-school graduates. Dramatic figures about functional illiteracy are cited along with employer complaints about the low level of skills that new graduates possess. The Center for Public Resources, in calling for a program to improve basic skill acquisition in schools, cited evidence that 44 percent of black youth leaving high school at age 18 cannot read above the fourth grade level, that scores on the Scholastic Aptitude Tests have been declining since the 1970s, and that the problem is compounded by the high number of school dropouts (1982, p. 2). Much black youth unemployment has been blamed on inadequate schooling. A U.S. General Accounting Office study (1982) summed up this view in its title, "Labor Market Problems of Teenagers Result Largely from Doing Poorly in School."

The level of attendance at public schools in general, and minority schools in particular, is also a serious problem. The New York City public school system, for example, admits to a 45 percent dropout rate between ninth grade and graduation; Calitri (1983) claims that the overall rate is even higher (68 percent), with a black dropout rate of 72 percent.

There is a natural potential tie between the stress on schools and industrial policy's emphasis on productivity and training. Industrial policy advocates concentrate on restoring productivity, which they feel can be accomplished more easily with a better educated work force. As we discussed earlier, the emphasis on declining education and skills is often coupled with an assertion that job requirements have risen dramatically; it is this "mismatch" between low skills and education and high demands of jobs that is seen to foster much black unemployment.

Although high levels of functional illiteracy and substantial school dropout are cause for serious concern, we question whether the mismatch analysis is an adequate explanation of black employment problems. The jobs that have grown the fastest in the U.S economy are not highly skilled jobs requiring much training. According to a recent Bureau of Labor Statistics forecast, there will be 19 million or so new jobs by 1990, 3.5 million of which will be professional and technical, a category that includes some menial low-skilled work but generally higher-paying jobs. Low-wage service and clerical work will account for almost 7 million new jobs.

Many analysts (for example, Kuttner 1983; McGahey 1983) have pointed out that most recent and projected job growth in the United States is concentrated in lower-skilled, lower-paying jobs, rather than technically demanding jobs with higher pay and higher skills. Rumberger found some evidence that overall skill requirements did increase between 1960 and 1976, "but at a slower rate than earlier periods" (1981, p. 578). In New York City, a leader in the transition from manufacturing to white-collar service work, the real skill demands of jobs have not changed in the last decade (Sullivan 1982). The problem remains, as many analysts point out, that there are simply not enough employment opportunities in urban areas. Human capital policy does not seem an adequate solution for this problem; although education and training are consistently associated with higher earnings, they are not consistent predictors of whether someone will find a job in the first place. And human capital programs by themselves do not create jobs.

The Changing Labor Market

The growth in the number of low-skilled jobs is a central issue for many industrial policy analysts. One solution envisioned is the growth in the high-tech sector. "High-tech" refers to both the production of highly sophisticated commodities and the use of highly sophisticated production techniques such as robots, computer-aided design (CAD), computer-aided manufacture (CAM), and the integration of all of these elements into flexible manufacturing systems (FMS). But high-tech enterprises do not necessarily require highly skilled labor. And since these processes are highly capital intensive, they tend to reduce the overall number of workers needed, while retraining smaller numbers of highly skilled workers.

The new labor demand generated by high-tech enterprises does not seem likely to take up the slack of workers displaced, much less provide substantial numbers of new jobs for the underemployed. Forecasts by the Bureau of Labor Statistics and by Data Resources, Inc. (DRI) show that in the next 10 years, high-tech jobs will replace less than half of the 2 million jobs lost in manufacturing in the last 3 years. And most jobs in high-tech industries will not be highly skilled. DRI estimates that fewer than one-third of the jobs will be for engineers and technicians; the remainder will be in traditional occupations (Business Week 28 March 1983).

Economist Ann Markusen has concluded that "dramatic employment growth" in high-tech "may be short-lived" and that the jobs created will not be stable blue-collar production work (1984, p. 8). Even traditional jobs are under the threat of displacement from high-tech. To cite one example, since 1973 DuPont has doubled its output capacity for synthetic fibers, but owing to mechanization and robotics the number of production workers required has risen only 4 or 5 percent (New York Times 16 May 1983).

This poses a dilemma for some advocates of industrial policy. Innovations such as those at DuPont dramatically raise productivity by integrating more sophisticated production technology, but they cut the number of jobs required in production in equally dramatic fashion. Unless the economy can boom in some unforeseen way, it is hard to see how enough labor demand will be generated to reemploy displaced industrial workers, much less hire those who are chronically unemployed. The U.S. Department of Labor (30 November 1984) has found that of 5.1 million workers who lost their jobs because of economic dislocation between 1979 and 1984, only 60 percent were reemployed when surveyed in 1984; over 40 percent of those with jobs in 1984 were earning less than they had in 1979. (Reich's stress on faster technical innovation and shifts to more specialized production, which requires fewer workers per unit of output, seems to ignore the problem of aggregate job growth.) The focus on generating aggregate economic growth through restoring productivity is thus problematic; the numbers and types of jobs that are likely to be generated will not meet the employment needs of many distressed Americans, especially minorities.

6. FUTURE POLICY OPTIONS

Several employment and training policy options emerge from the industrial policy debate. In this section, we comment on their implications for minorities and on the role of more traditional policies, such as affirmative action.

Retraining Policy and Displaced Workers

One of the central themes of industrial policy involves the retraining of workers displaced by economic changes. This policy is also advocated in different form through the Reagan administration's Job Training Partnership Act, which has a separate title for displaced workers.

Retraining implies that someone had a previous job; it does nothing for the long-term unemployed. Further, most retraining models concentrate on large primary firms and often involve union cooperation. Minority workers are at risk in these firms, as they often have less seniority than white workers--and retraining alone will not create new jobs. Industrial layoffs have hit minorities in certain firms and industries especially hard. When Atari, Inc., laid off 1,700 production workers while moving production to Asian plants, union organizers claimed that Latinos and Asians made up almost 80 percent of those laid off. According to the United Auto Workers, layoffs in the auto industry alone accounted for a 1 percent drop in the national average income for blacks (Los Angeles Times 2 June 1983).

Minorities in the secondary labor market face even bigger obstacles in obtaining meaningful training and job placement. Small firms are even less likely than large ones to administer training programs or find new jobs for redundant workers. The lack of unionization for many workers in small firms means that there are no institutions to coordinate retraining and transitional services.

A final concern is that retraining funds may be taken up by more politically powerful primary workers displaced from major unionized industries. Indeed, some analysts endorse this as an explicit goal. Harvard economist D. Quinn Mills, in a 1981 conference on industrial policy, stated:

> It is time to loosen the connection between training and job placement activities and the disadvantaged, and to redirect public employment and training efforts to a broader segment of the population. . . . Funds are scarce for large-scale public programs to assist the unemployed. Should there be a reallocation of effort from the disadvantaged to the industrially displaced? The answer is yes. Training and relocation programs have done only limited good for the disadvantaged. They promise a far higher payoff with the industrially displaced. (1983, pp. 276-77)

Mills's endorsement of shifting resources from the disadvantaged is not explicitly adopted by any advocate of industrial policy. But the stress on increasing interfirm and geographic mobility of workers through retraining programs and on administering these programs through firms and unions runs the danger of leaving many blacks out of retraining programs. Reich stresses that the costs of adjustment should not fall too heavily on blacks, but the policies that he has advocated thus far do not directly address this problem.*

Retraining, in any case, may be of little value if the real problem is too few jobs. Retraining policy extends the mismatch analysis to workers who have been steadily employed; as they cannot be said to have bad work habits or attitudes, the analysis concentrates on their obsolete skills. But displaced workers are often removed from their jobs by the very factor called for in industrial policy: increased productivity through technical innovations in production and capital substitution. Mills notes that such "reindustrialization" may only slow the loss of manufacturing work without adding any new jobs (1983, p. 264).

---

* Our focus here is on a subset of unionized workers--production workers in blue-collar primary industries. Although blacks are unionized in many sectors, including public employment, health care, and some secondary labor-market sectors, the political power of nonindustrial unions in fighting for retraining funds is relatively weak when compared to unionized workers who have primary jobs in sectors like steel, automobiles, and construction.

A more jaundiced view of retraining is that workers will simply be removed from the labor market for some period of time, while participating in programs. In this view, retraining programs will perform one of the latent functions of all schooling--keeping people out of the job market. Retraining may also be coupled with receipt of transfer payments.

Some analyses suggest that the real barrier to displaced workers' finding new jobs is the workers' reluctance to accept work that pays substantially less than their previous jobs (Business Week 19 September 1983). Many retraining programs feature group meetings for displaced workers, parts of which consist of "reality therapy"--getting workers to accept that their futures have changed--and then teaching them how to obtain jobs, fill out resumes, make calls on employers, and so on.*

David Swinton has criticized the retraining thrust of current policy, claiming that the real problem is that "there are not enough jobs to fully employ those people who want to work. By training people in the absence of jobs, we will train people who remain unemployed, or the trained will displace the untrained" (Los Angeles Times 2 June 1983). In the face of the weak projections for new jobs in technically sophisticated work and the possibilities of technological displacement in manufacturing and services, advocates of retraining must address the question of where new jobs will come from. Will the microeconomic effects of productivity and management changes produce new jobs? In what industries, occupations, and regions of the country? It may be entirely possible to get rises in productivity without substantial overall gains in output and without creating new employment. In this situation, what will displaced workers do? And what is the role of retraining policy for those in the secondary labor market, especially those who are chronically unemployed? Mills's frank endorsement of shifting resources away from the disadvantaged to displaced industrial workers raises a grim vision of competition among different groups of the unemployed for increasingly limited government funds.

Infrastructure Rebuilding and Public-Service Employment

Some industrial policy programs, notably those proposed by Rohatyn (1983), involve substantial commitments to rebuild the

* Ironically, these methods, now extended to prime-age industrial workers, are the same as those directed at chronically unemployed minorities in the 1970s.

infrastructure in cities, especially in declining older urban areas. This may hold some promise for black employment, but its possibilities would be enhanced by expanding government hiring. The public sector accounted for much improvement in black employment during the 1970s. Rumberger estimates that, in 1980, 35 percent of black males and 45 percent of black females owed their jobs either directly or indirectly to government spending; 54 percent of black male college graduates and fully 72 percent of black female graduates had jobs attributable to federal spending (1983, Table 5).

And black college-educated professionals were not the only ones to benefit from an expanding public sector; short-term public-service employment also aided less-educated blacks. Ellwood and Wise found that the Federal Summer Youth Employment Program (SYEP) provided almost 45 percent of all summer jobs for minority youth aged 14-19 in July 1978; 3 percent of white jobs were due to the program. Fifty percent of white youths had private-sector non-SYEP jobs, while only 18 percent of minority youth did (1983, pp. 56-62).

Infrastructure programs may not provide extraordinary assistance to black men, since blacks hold less skilled and less high-paying jobs than whites in sectors such as construction, but they are still important. During 1981, blacks and other minorities represented 8.1 percent of all construction workers and 12.8 percent of transportation and public utility workers, while making up 11.6 percent of the employed work force (U.S. Department of Labor, Employment and Earnings March 1982).

For public employment to improve the jobs of females, expanded social service employment would be required, a policy not mentioned by most industrial policy advocates. Expanded social services are a double bonus for women, as women both work in and are the major recipients of many services such as day care and expanded education. The emphasis on better schooling thus may provide opportunities for black college-educated women as teachers and for others as school support personnel.

Public-service employment has been roundly criticized by many, but it remains an important source of employment for blacks and other minorities. Males would stand to benefit from expanded infrastructure repair and a vigorous affirmative action program in hiring and contracting. Females would not benefit from infrastructure construction to any great extent, although a program of repair and maintenance of public facilities might provide some jobs for them. But expanded day care, health programs, education, and other such services would have double advantages for females, especially minorities. So increasing infrastructure repair and expanding social services in industrial policy programs would be a strong advantage for blacks.

Affirmative Action and Direct Government Intervention

Policies to aid blacks cannot ignore affirmative action and other forms of direct governmental intervention. Evidence suggests that affirmative action in hiring and in contracting has had positive effects on black employment. Economist Jonathan Leonard (1984a, 1984b) has concluded that federal affirmative action programs increased the employment of minorities and also significantly raised their wages, especially when the programs were vigorously enforced and combined with skill training. Federal antidiscrimination activity is found by some researchers to be the most likely explanation for improvement in the black-to-white earnings ratio for some segments of the population (e.g., college-educated young) since 1964 (Brown 1981), and other analyses (summarized by Freeman) show that federal contractors, especially those facing compliance reviews, have larger increases in black employment than other firms (1982b, p. 5).

Further, this sort of protection seems necessary to protect the gains blacks have made, even in government jobs. Although black employment gains were substantial in an expanding public sector, the current shrinkage of government is causing rapid reversals of those gains. Federal agencies dismissed minorities at a rate 50 percent greater than that for whites in 1981; the number of layoffs doubled in 1982, hitting upper-level black professionals hardest (New York Times 17 September 1983).

Of course, governmental programs might also have negative impacts. The minimum wage and welfare policies, in particular, have been examined for their negative effects on black employment. However, economic research has found that such negative effects tend to be "moderate or modest," not overwhelming (Freeman 1982b, pp. 2-3).

In recent years, conservative critics have launched a broader attack on welfare programs. Analysts such as Walter Williams, Thomas Sowell, and Charles Murray have argued that American welfare programs not only fail to assist blacks and other economically distressed people, but also make the distressed worse off by perpetuating a culture of dependency. Murray, in Losing Ground (1984), advocated the elimination of virtually all federal means-tested social programs--food stamps, AFDC, and the like--arguing that the rise in these programs coincided with worsening conditions for blacks and that the programs both fostered dependency and stifled economic growth. He stated that economic growth would aid poor blacks more than any targeted social programs would.

In fact, critics on the left have themselves attacked poverty programs for fostering dependency (Piven and Cloward 1971). The peculiar configuration of the American welfare state has kept most transfer payment programs, especially Great Society initiatives, separate from economic development goals (Skocpol and Ikenberry 1983). But it seems a leap to conclude that poverty programs **cause** continued economic distress for blacks. Proponents of such programs conclude just the opposite; if black conditions have become worse, then more funding is required.

We are not persuaded that welfare state programs are a significant cause of America's economic troubles. Many welfare state programs in the United States should, however, be redesigned with more emphasis on economic growth, social equity, and community economic development (Jeffries and McGahey, forthcoming). As Robert Kuttner (1984) has pointed out, in the 1970s many European countries had both faster economic growth and greater social equality than the United States. While Europe's economic growth in the 1970s is perhaps less compelling when we compare recent U.S. economic growth to current stagnation in Europe, our recent economic growth has gone hand-in-hand with growing social inequality and historically high levels of unemployment. Although economic growth is necessary for improving the lives of economically distressed Americans, it does not seem to be a sufficient reason for tolerating social inequality and high levels of black unemployment.

But welfare programs--particularly income maintenance--have little or no political support, except in the form of unemployment insurance or Social Security, programs not usually perceived as transfer programs. Americans traditionally dislike income redistribution schemes, preferring to pin their hopes for social mobility on education (DeLeone 1979). For this reason, any expansion of income maintenance will have more support if it is tied to work or training programs, even if those programs (like many of their predecessors) do not substantially raise the labor-market returns of their participants.

Minority Participation in Industrial Policy

This paper has discussed a wide range of issues surrounding the industrial policy debate, but the primary concern has been the employment problems of minority workers and the role of education and training policies in solving those problems. Thus far, industrial policy advocates have said very little about the particular problems of black and minority workers. Most express laudable sentiments for equalizing the burdens of economic adjustment, but the major stress in industrial policy remains on restoring economic growth through increasing productivity. They encourage growth through a variety of methods, including better foreign trade policy, increased retraining of laid-off workers, closer ties between schools and training, on the one hand, and the needs of the private labor market, on the other hand, and encouragement of economic revival in central cities through a combination of incentives to private firms and construction of public works.

What strikes us about this list is not its novelty, but its familiarity. Economic policies aimed at disadvantaged workers throughout the 1960s and 1970s had exactly the same kinds of things on their agendas (although with somewhat less attention to foreign trade issues), from the earliest days of manpower policy through the War on Poverty in the 1960s, through CETA in the 1970s, and up to the latest programs of the Reagan administration. The programs now endorsed by industrial policy proponents sound rather similar. The one goal most of them back away from, with the exception of some critics on the left, is direct income stabilization policy. Most prefer to link income stabilization to participation in the labor market or training; in more extreme cases, some endorse diverting resources from the traditionally disadvantaged to the recently displaced.

It may be that human capital policies such as those advocated by Reich will in fact spur new economic growth and somehow provide enough new jobs to absorb both the disadvantaged and the displaced. But we are not optimistic about this possibility. Service and high-tech enterprises so far seem to have widened earnings gaps, not narrowed them. Many of the new jobs anticipated in the next decade will require few skills, and there may be increased competition for those jobs.

Certainly better schooling, especially in math and language basics, is a desirable social goal in itself. The goal of preparing workers to be more flexible in the labor market is, in fact, more likely to be enhanced by general educational development than by occupation-specific or employer-based training. But poor economic performance for many individuals, especially minorities, is unlikely to be addressed adequately by human capital policies alone. If the scenario of raised productivity with low employment and earnings growth is played out--a scenario that seems quite possible--other sorts of policies may have to be considered. These might include a more active and permanent role for public-service employment, national wage and price policies to restrain inflation, reorganization of work with earlier retirement and work sharing, a greater role for communities in directing economic activity through such programs as producer's cooperatives in cities, and the like.

We do not attempt to develop an alternative agenda in this paper. But we are concerned that, once again, the employment problems of minorities (and increasing numbers of white Americans) are being defined largely in terms of a mismatch between their inadequate skills and education and the allegedly high skills demanded by a changing labor-market structure. And we fear that liberals and conservatives alike have assumed that the distinctive employment problems of minority workers will be solved by general economic growth. Growth alone did not solve the black employment problems of the sixties and seventies (Harris 1983), and there is now depressing evidence that the black economic situation is deteriorating even as the U.S economy grows.

Restoring growth, especially through productivity gains driven by capital substitution, may not in and of itself provide much help for blacks in the eighties and future decades. Adjustment policies certainly will be required in the future, but we foresee a continuing need for affirmative action programs, public employment, and income redistribution policies. It is manifestly harder to endorse such policies at a time when overall economic prospects remain so uncertain; like many industrial policy advocates, we do not minimize the political problems with such an agenda. But we hope that this paper will help stimulate a dialogue between industrial policy advocates and minority leaders, for any change in the American economy that smacks of increased planning or further politicization of the distribution of economic resources will surely require the active participation of both.

REFERENCES

AFL-CIO. "Statements Adopted by the Executive Council." Boston, August 8-10, 1983.

Aho, C. Michael, and J. A. Orr. "Trade-Sensitive Employment: Who Are The Affected Workers?" Monthly Labor Review 104 (February 1981).

Alperovitz, Gar, and Jeff Faux. Rebuilding America: A Blueprint for the New Economy. New York: Pantheon, 1984.

Becker, Gary S. Human Capital. 2d ed. Chicago: University of Chicago Press, 1975.

Black Enterprise. "BE Board of Economists Report: Unemployment," March 1983.

Bluestone, Barry, and B. Harrison. The Deindustrialization of America. New York: Basic Books, 1982.

Borjas, George. "The Demographic Determinants of the Demand for Black Labor." Paper prepared for the Conference on Inner City Black Youth Unemployment, National Bureau of Economic Research, Cambridge, MA, 1983.

Bowles, Samuel, D. Gordon, and T. E. Weisskopf. Beyond the Wasteland: A Democratic Alternative to Economic Decline. Garden City, NY: Anchor Press/Doubleday, 1983a.

________. "'Industrial Policy'--Now the Bad News." The Nation 4 (June 1983b): 236.

Brown, Charles. "The Federal Attack on Labor Market Discrimination: The Mouse That Roared." Working paper no. 664, National Bureau of Economic Research, Cambridge, MA, 1981.

Business Week. "America Rushes To High Tech For Growth," 28 March 1983, pp. 84-98.

________. "Industrial Policy: Is It The Answer?" 4 July 1983, pp. 54-62.

________. "Displaced Workers May Have to Face Lower Wages," 19 September 1983, p. 22.

________. "The Furor Over America's Ability to Compete," 10 September 1984, pp. 89-90.

Calitri, Ronald. "Minority Secondary Education in New York State and New York City." Aspira of New York, Inc., New York, 1983.

Center for Labor and Urban Programs Research and Analysis. "Young People in the New York Labor Market." Queens College, City University of New York, New York, 1981.

Center For Public Resources. Basic Skills in the U.S. Work Force. New York: Center For Public Resources, 1982.

Clark, Kim B., and L. H. Summers. "The Dynamics of Youth Unemployment." Working paper no. 274, National Bureau of Economic Research, Cambridge, MA, 1978.

________. "Labor Market Dynamics and Unemployment: A Reconsideration." Brookings Papers on Economic Activity, no. 1 (1979).

Cogan, John F. "The Decline in Black Teenage Employment: 1950-1970." American Economic Review, September 1982, pp. 621-38.

Cook, Robert F., V. L. Rawlins, C. J. Reesman, K. Rupp, and W. M. Turnage. State Level Implementation of the job Training Partnership Act. Rockville, MD: Westat, May 1984.

Culp, Jerome, and B. Dunson. "Brothers of a Different Color: A Preliminary Look at Employer Treatment of White and Black Youth." Paper prepared for the Conference on Inner City Black Youth Unemployment, National Bureau of Economic Research, Cambridge, MA, 1983.

Danziger, Sheldon, R. Haveman, and R. Plotnick. "Retrenchment or Reorientation: Options for Income Support Policy."

Discussion paper 597-80, Institute for Research on Poverty, University of Wisconsin, Madison, WI, March 1980.

Datcher-Loury, Linda, and G. Loury. "The Effects of Attitudes and Aspirations on the Labor Supply of Young Black Men." Paper prepared for the Conference on Inner City Black Youth Unemployment, National Bureau of Economic Research, Cambridge, MA, 1983.

DeLeone, Richard H. Small Futures: Children, Inequality, and the Limits of Liberal Reform. New York: Harcourt Brace Jovanovich, 1979.

Denison, Edward F. Accounting For Slower Economic Growth. Washington, DC: The Brookings Institution, 1979.

Doeringer, Peter B. "Programs to Employ the Disadvantaged: A Labor Market Perspective." In Programs to Employ the Disadvantaged, ed. P. Doeringer. Englewood Cliffs, NJ: Prentice Hall, 1969.

Eckstein, Otto, C. Caton, R. Brinner, and P. Duprey. The DRI Report on U.S. Manufacturing Industries. New York: McGraw-Hill, 1984.

Ellwood, David T. "Teenage Unemployment: Permanent Scars of Temporary Blemishes." Working paper no. 399, National Bureau of Economic Research, Cambridge, MA, 1979.

_____________. "The Spatial Mismatch Hypothesis: Are There Teenage Jobs Missing in the Ghetto?" Paper prepared for the Conference on Inner City Black Youth Unemployment, National Bureau of Economic Research, Cambridge, MA, 1983.

Ellwood, David T., and D. Wise. "Youth Employment in the Seventies: The Changing Circumstances of Young Adults." Working paper no. 1055, National Bureau of Economic Research, Cambridge, MA, 1983.

Freeman, Richard B. "Why Is There a Youth Labor Market Problem?" In Youth Employment and Public Policy, ed. Bernard E. Anderson and I. Sawhill. Englewood Cliffs, NJ: Prentice-Hall, 1978.

____________. "The Evolution of the American Labor Market." In The American Economy in Transition, ed. Martin Feldstein. Chicago: University of Chicago Press, 1980.

__________. "Troubled Workers in the Labor Market." Discussion paper no. 881, Harvard Institute For Economic Research, Cambridge, MA, 1982a.

__________. "Program Report: Labor Studies." NBER Reporter (National Bureau of Economic Research) (Summer 1982b): 1-6.

__________. "Who Escapes? The Relation of Church-Going and Other Background Factors to the Socio-Economic Performance of Black Male Youths from Inner-City Poverty Tracts." Paper prepared for the Conference on Inner City Black Youth Unemployment, National Bureau of Economic Research, Cambridge, MA, 1983.

Grant, James H. "Education, Training and Labor Market Performance of Youths Out of School." Paper prepared for the Conference on Inner City Black Youth Unemployment, National Bureau of Economic Research, Cambridge, MA, 1983.

Guttman, Robert. "Job Training Partnership Act: New Help for the Unemployed." Monthly Labor Review 106 (March 1983).

Hall, Robert. "Turnover in the Labor Force." Brookings Papers on Economic Activity, no. 3 (1972).

Harris, Donald J. "Economic Growth, Structural Change, and the Relative Income Status of Blacks in the U.S. Economy, 1947-78." Review of Black Political Economy 12 (Spring 1983): 75-92.

Harrison, Bennett. Education, Training, and the Urban Ghetto. Baltimore: The Johns Hopkins University Press, 1972.

Haveman, Robert H. A Decade of Federal Antipoverty Programs. New York: Academic Press, 1979.

Hewitt, William B. "Manpower Revenue Sharing--The Administration's Outlook." Good Governance 90 (Fall 1973).

Jeffries, John M., and R. McGahey. "Equity, Growth and Change: Anti-Discrimination Policy in an Era of Economic Transformation." Review of Law and Social Change, forthcoming.

Kuttner, Robert. "The Declining Middle." The Atlantic Monthly, July 1983, pp. 60-72.

______________. The Economic Illusion: False Choices Between Prosperity and Social Justice. Boston: Houghton-Mifflin, 1984.

Lawrence, Robert Z. Can America Compete? Washington, DC: The Brookings Institution, 1984.

Leonard, Jonathan S. "Employment and Occupational Advance Under Affirmative Action." Working paper no. 1270, National Bureau of Economic Research, Cambridge, MA, 1984a.

______________. "The Impact of Affirmative Action on Employment." Working paper no. 1310, National Bureau of Economic Research, Cambridge, MA, 1984b.

Levitan, Sar, and Garth L. Mangum. Federal Training and Work Programs in the Sixties. Ann Arbor, MI: Institute of Labor and Industrial Relations, University of Michigan/Wayne State University, 1969.

Los Angeles Times. "Layoffs of Minorities Are Disproportionate," 2 June 1983.

McGahey, Richard M. "Labor Market Structure, the Economic Choice Model, and Crime." Paper presented at the annual meeting of the American Economic Association, Washington, DC, December 1981.

______________. "Labor Market Segmentation, Human Capital, and the Economics of Crime." Ph.D. dissertation, New School for Social Research, 1982.

______________. "High Tech, Low Hopes." New York Sunday Times, Op-Ed Section, 15 May 1983.

Magaziner, Ira C., and R. B. Reich. Minding America's Business: The Decline and Rise of the American Economy. New York: Random House, Vintage Books, 1983.

Mangum, Garth L. The Emergence of Manpower Policy. New York: Holt, Rinehart and Winston, 1969.

Mangum, Garth L., and John Walsh. A Decade of Manpower Development and Training. Salt Lake City, UT: Olympus, 1973.

Manpower Demonstration Research Corporation. Summary and Findings of the National Supported Work Demonstration. Cambridge, MA: Ballinger, 1981.

Manpower Report of the President. Washington, DC: U.S. Government Printing Office, various years.

Marable, Manning. From the Grassroots: Social and Political Essays Towards Afro-American Liberation. Boston: South End Press, 1980.

Markusen, Ann R. "High Technology and the Future of Employment." Paper presented at the National Conference on Economic Dislocation and Job Loss, Washington, DC, April 1984.

Marth, Del. "The Job Training Partnership Act: A Victory For Business--And A Challenge." Nation's Business 71 (January 1983).

Mills, D. Quinn. "The Human Resource Consequences of Industrial Revitalization." In Toward a New U.S. Industrial Policy? ed. Michael L. Wachter and Susan M. Wachter. Philadelphia: University of Pennsylvania Press, 1983, pp. 257-80.

Mirengoff, William, and L. Rindler. CETA: Manpower Programs Under Local Control. Washington, DC: National Academy of Sciences, 1978.

Mondale, Walter F. Excerpts from a speech delivered to the AFL-CIO Industrial Union Department Legislative Conference, 4 May 1983.

Montgomery, Edward, and P. Jackson. "Layoffs, Discharges, and Youth Unemployment." Paper presented for the Conference on Inner City Black Youth Unemployment, National Bureau of Economic Research, Cambridge, MA, 1983.

Murray, Charles A. Losing Ground: American Social Policy, 1950-1980. New York: Basic Books, 1984.

New York Times. "Few on Layoffs May be Rehired; U.S. Push in World Market Urged," 16 May 1983, sec. 1, p. A1.

______________. "Battling to Stem the Black Layoff Tide." 17 September 1983.

______________. "'High Tech' No Jobs Panacea, Experts Say," 18 September 1983, sec. 1, p. A1.

Osterman, Paul. Getting Started: The Youth Labor Market. Cambridge, MA: The MIT Press, 1980.

Parnes, Herbert D. Unemployment Experiences of Individuals Over a Decade. Kalamazoo, MI: W. E. Upjohn Institute for Employment Research, 1982.

Patterson, Orlando. Ethnic Chauvinism: The Reactionary Response. New York: Stein and Day, 1977.

Piore, Michael J. "The Dual Labor Market: Theory and Implications." In Problems in Political Economy: An Urban Perspective, ed. David M. Gordon. Lexington, MA: D.C. Heath, 1977.

Piven, Frances Fox, and R. A. Cloward. Regulating the Poor: The Functions of Public Welfare. New York: Pantheon, 1971.

Proctor, James. "Racial Pressures on Urban Institutions." In The Campus and the Racial Crisis, ed. Daniel C. Nichols and Olive Mills. Washington, DC: American Council on Education, 1970.

Reich, Robert B. "Industrial Evolution." Democracy 3 (Summer 1983a): 10-20.

________. The Next American Frontier. New York: The New York Times Book Co., Inc., 1983b.

Rohatyn, Felix. "Time For A Change." New York Review of Books, 18 August 1983, pp. 46-49.

Rumberger, Russell W. "The Employment Impact of Government Spending." Institute for Research on Educational Finance and Governance, School of Education, Stanford University, Palo Alto, CA, May 1983.

________. "The Changing Skill Requirements of Jobs in the U.S. Economy." Industrial and Labor Relations Review 34 (July 1981): 578-90.

Rustin, Bayard. "From Protest to Politics: The Future of the Civil Rights Movement." Commentary 39 (February 1965).

Sadd, Susan, M. Kotkin, and S. R. Friedman. "Alternative Youth Employment Strategies Project: Final Report." Vera Institute of Justice, New York, 1983.

Sawhill, Isabel V. "Remarks." In The Business Sector Role In Employment Policy. National Commission for Manpower Policy, special report no. 31, November 1978.

Skocpol, Theda, and J. Ikenberry. "The Political Formation of the American Welfare State." Comparative Social Research 6 (1983): 87-148.

Stevenson, Wayne. "The Transition from School to Work." In The Lingering Crisis of Youth Unemployment, ed. Arvil V. Adams and G. Mangum. Kalamazoo, MI: W. E. Upjohn Institute for Employment Research, 1978.

Sullivan, Eileen. "Promising Occupations and Industries," New York City Department of Employment, New York, 1982.

Sullivan, Mercer. "The Two Youth Crime Problems." New York Affairs 8, no. 1 (1983).

Swinton, David. "The Economic Status of the Black Population." In The State of Black America, 1983. New York: National Urban League, 1983.

U.S. Bureau of the Census. America's Black Population: A Statistical View, 1970-1982. Washington, DC: U.S Government Printing Office, 1983.

U.S. Commission on Civil Rights. Unemployment and Underemployment Among Blacks, Hispanics, and Women. Clearinghouse Publication 74. Washington, DC: U.S. Government Printing Office, 1982.

U.S. Congress. House. Committee on Banking, Finance, and Urban Affairs. Subcommittee on Economic Stabilization. Industrial Policy: Hearings. 98th Congress, 1st and 2nd sessions, June 1983-January 1984.

U.S. Congress. House. Committee on Education and Labor. National Employment Priorities Act, H.R. 2847. 98th Congress, 1st session, 1983.

U.S. Department of Labor, Bureau of Labor Statistics. BLS Reports on Displaced Workers. USDL 84-492, Washington, DC, November 1984.

____________. Employment and Earnings, various editions.

U.S. General Accounting Office. Labor Market Problems of Teenagers Result Largely From Doing Poorly in School. Washington, DC: U.S. Government Printing Office, 1982.

U.S. National Advisory Commission on Civil Disorders. Report of the National Advisory Commmission on Civil Disorders. Washington, DC: U.S. Government Printing Office, 1968.

U.S. Statutes At Large, 1964. Vol. 78. Washington, DC: U.S. Government Printing Office, 1965.

Walker, Gary, W. Grinker, T. Seessel, R. C. Smith, and V. Cama. An Independent Sector Assessment of the Job Training Partnership Act. Phase I: The Initial Transition. New York: Grinker, Walker, and Associates, March 1984.

Westcott, Diane N. "Blacks in the 1970s: Did They Scale the Job Ladder?" Monthly Labor Review 105 (June 1982).

ABOUT THE AUTHORS

Richard M. McGahey is a research associate at the Urban Research Center of New York University. Previously, he was a deputy project director at the Vera Institute of Justice. He is the author of several articles and reports on labor markets.

John M. Jeffries, also a research associate at the Urban Research Center, has been a research associate at Cornell University and a research assistant at the Brookings Institution. He has also served as a staff economist at the Public Agenda Foundation in New York.

The authors wish to thank the A. Phillip Randolph Foundation and the Charles H. Revson Foundation for supporting the study; Susan Sheehan Wieler of the Urban Research Center for her research assistance; Linda Wheeler, Susan Sebbard, and Karren Moore for their manuscript preparation; Catherine Iino and Constance Toliver of the Joint Center for their editorial services; and Edwin Dorn and Eddie Williams of the Joint Center for their helpful comments.

SELECTED JCPS PUBLICATIONS

Black Americans and the Shaping of U.S. Foreign Policy: Proceedings of a JCPS Roundtable, 1981. ISBN 0-941410-18-8. $4.95

Black Elected Officials and their Constituencies, Thomas E. Cavanagh and Denise Stockton, 1983. ISBN 0-941410-28-5. $4.95.

Black Elected Officials: A National Roster, 1985. Available from UNIPUB, P.O. Box 1222, Ann Arbor, MI 48106. $27.50.

Black Employment in City Government, 1973-1980, Peter Eisinger, 1983. ISBN 0-941410-32-3. $4.95.

Blacks and the 1984 Democratic National Convention: A Guide, (Election '84 Report No. 3), 1984. ISBN 0-941410-46-3. $4.95.

Blacks and the 1984 Republican National Convention: A Guide, (Election '84 Report No. 4), 1984. ISBN 0-941410-51-X. $4.95.

Blacks on the Move: A Decade of Demographic Change, William P. O'Hare, Jane-yu Li, Roy Chatterjee, and Margaret Shukur, abridged by Phillip Sawicki, 1982. ISBN 0-941410-25-0. $4.95.

The Changing Patterns of Black Family Income, 1960-1982, Henry E. Felder, 1984. ISBN 0-941410-43-9. $4.95.

Energy and Equity: Some Social Concerns, edited by Ellis Cose, 1979. ISBN 0-941410-09-9. $8.50.

Focus, JCPS monthly newsletter. ISSN 0740-0195. $12.00 per annum.

Foreign Trade Policy and Black Economic Advancement: Proceedings of a JCPS Roundtable, 1981. ISBN 0-941410-19-6. $4.95.

How to Use Section 5 of the Voting Rights Act, third edition, Barbara Y. Phillips, 1984. ISBN 0-941410-27-7. $4.95.

The Impact of the Black Electorate (Election '84 Report No. 1), Thomas E. Cavanagh, 1984. ISBN 0-941410-44-7. $4.95.

The JCPS Congressional District Fact Book, edited by Thomas E. Cavanagh, 1984. ISBN 0-941410-34-X. $5.95.

Jesse Jackson's Campaign: The Primaries and Caucuses (Election '84 Report No. 2), Thomas E. Cavanagh and Lorn S. Foster, 1984. ISBN 0-941410-45-5. $4.95.

Minority Vote Dilution, edited by Chandler Davidson, 1984. Available from Howard University Press, 2900 Van Ness St., Washington, DC 20008. $24.95.

Mobilizing the Black Community: The Effects of Personal Contact Campaigning on Black Voters, Paul Carton, 1984. ISBN 0-941410-42-0. $4.95

The Nineteen Eighties: Prologue and Prospect, Kenneth B. Clark and John Hope Franklin, 1981. ISBN 0-941410-20-X. $2.95.

A Policy Framework for Racial Justice, (statement by thirty black scholars), 1983. Introduction by Kenneth B. Clark and John Hope Franklin. ISBN 0-941410-30-7. $4.95.

Public School Desegregation in the United States, 1968-1980, Gary Orfield, 1983. ISBN 0-941410-29-3. $4.95.

Race and Political Strategy, edited by Thomas E. Cavanagh, 1983. ISBN 0-941410-33-1. $4.95.

Thirty Years after Brown, Jennifer L. Hochschild, 1985. ISBN 0-941410-49-8. $4.95.

Vote Dilution, Minority Voting Rights, and the Courts, Stephen L. Wasby, 1982. ISBN 0-941410-22-6. $4.95.

The Voting Rights Act and Black Electoral Participation, Kenneth H. Thompson, 1982. ISBN 0-941410-24-2. $4.95.

Wealth and Economic Status: A Perspective on Racial Inequity, by William P. O'Hare, 1983. ISBN 0-941410-35-8. $4.95.